Little Me Can Live
A Big Life

Integrating Paradoxes For Change

PETER ALLMAN

iUniverse, Inc.
New York   Bloomington

Little Me Can Live A Big Life
Integrating Paradoxes For Change

iUniverse books may be ordered through booksellers or by contacting:

iUniverse
1663 Liberty Drive
Bloomington, IN 47403
www.iuniverse.com
1-800-Authors (1-800-288-4677)

Because of the dynamic nature of the Internet, any Web addresses or links contained in this book may have changed since publication and may no longer be valid. The views expressed in this work are solely those of the author and do not necessarily reflect the views of the publisher, and the publisher hereby disclaims any responsibility for them.

ISBN: 978-1-4401-3505-7 (sc)
ISBN: 978-1-4401-3506-4 (ebook)

Printed in the United States of America

iUniverse rev. date: 4/27/2009

For Maureen

Contents

Integrating Mind, Body, Spirit

Introduction

What is a paradox? How will embracing paradoxes help *Little Me Live a Big Life?*

From ancient Greek mythology to modern literature and movies, stories are shared about the hero's journey. These tales are about breaking out of a small, limited life, getting to know yourself better, slaying the dragons (your personal issues), and finding the truths of life which will ultimately lead to freedom and a bigger life. Many, many truths will help us grow both psychologically (our humanness from God) and spiritually (our divinity from God). By learning and integrating paradoxical truths, you will more fully honor your own hero's journey.

Webster defines paradox as "A statement that is seemingly contradictory or opposed to common sense and yet is perhaps true." A paradox embraces "both-and" thinking instead of "either-or" thinking. For example, I am both strong and weak. I am both a saint and a sinner. I am both generous and selfish. I both laugh and cry. Paradoxes are two ends of the same continuum. They are interdependent and co-exist with one another. Each depends upon the other for meaning (you cannot understand night without day).

Modern culture has a difficult time accepting this paradigm. We are much more comfortable with the dualistic "either-or" mentality of this quote from Popeye: "You're either with me or you're against me." Western culture likes to put people and experiences in boxes. For example, are you conservative or liberal, blue-collar or white-collar? Is this right or wrong, pleasurable or painful? This black and white, dualistic, dichotomized thinking will keep us stuck and unable to grow into the bigger life for which we were created. For example, western thinking has separated and dichotomized the body and the mind. This has created and prolonged many illnesses. We know that the mind and the body are united, interconnected, and have an intricate relationship in each person.

Philosophers in ancient China created a theory based on the construct of two polar complements, called Yin and Yang. These opposite qualities exist in relation to each other. Their ancient wisdom stated that no entity could ever be isolated from its relationship to its opposite or other entities. All things are seen as parts of a whole. Yin and Yang can be distinguished, but they cannot be separated. They depend on each other and they function in relation to each other. There is synergy when paradoxes are involved, because the polarity has been harnessed.

When conflict is seen as an either-or dilemma, hurt feelings, anger, and a loser emerge. Instead of seeing conflict being resolved in a win-lose scenario, we would do much better, both for our individual health and for the health of our society, if we resolved conflict in terms of both-and thinking, which would (paradoxically) create a win-win solution. Each side can be enhanced by working out differences.

Dr. Steven Sample, tenth president of the University of Southern California, writes about a counter-intuitive practice of "thinking gray." Either-or thinking is putting things in black or white categories. Both-and thinking blends those two colors together and makes gray. Many people are proud to think in absolutes and believe it takes strength to stand firm on the "black" or "white" side of the continuum. In fact, it takes more fortitude to see both sides, and embrace the paradox of the "grayness" of life. Paradoxically, life is then experienced in Technicolor!

Paradoxes are a strange and mysterious twoness. They may not make sense to our rational minds. In fact, paradoxes disturb our conventional way of thinking. Paradoxes can give a jolt that pushes us out of being stuck and into freedom.

Embracing paradoxes is the art of balancing opposites. It is not canceling each other out, but maintaining a healthy tension between the two. For example, entering into an exercise program will be *both* painful *and* pleasurable. By being conscious of both dynamics, we might actually exercise because we know the pain will pass and we will soon feel the pleasure of a body that is in better shape.

Composers use both major *and* minor keys to write their musical masterpieces. Using either one key or the other creates simple tunes. Symphonies, in their harmonious complexity, are created by using both keys.

The arts are full of unresolved paradoxical characters. Robert Louis Stevenson's 1886 novel, *The Strange Case of Dr. Jekyll and Mr. Hyde* is a splendid example of enlightening us to the "both-and" nature of humankind. Stevenson shows how each of us has an inner conflict of good and evil. Another illustrative example is one of George Lucas' main characters in *Star Wars*, Darth Vader. His birth name was Anakin Skywalker. He was a bright, kind, selfless child. He had an innate connection to the Force which allowed him to accomplish many things beyond his age. After his mother was killed, Anakin slowly embraced the Dark Side. Redemption occurred at the end when he admitted to Luke that the good within him was not destroyed after all. Finally, the character of Gollum in *The Lord of the Rings: The Two Towers,* has Shakespearean complexity. He has an inner conflict between the innocent Hobbit (Sméagol) he once was and the immoral and devious fiend he has become. The director Peter Jackson evokes these contradictory traits to create an interesting, paradoxical character.

The renowned psychologist Carl Jung said, "Only the paradox comes anywhere near to comprehending the fullness of life." We relate to the Jekyll/Hyde, Anakin/Darth Vader, and Gollum/Sméagol characters because we know at a deep level that both sides are facets of humanity. They are wound together indivisibly in us. How comfortable do you feel with your own contradictions? This awareness allows us to resolve the paradox by more fully choosing what we want to manifest.

When J.K. Rowling penned the ending of Harry Potter's journey, she said, "I've never felt such a mixture of extreme emotions in my life, never dreamed I could feel simultaneously heartbroken and euphoric." Poet Maya Angelou stated when she is ready to write, a clean sheet of paper scares and thrills her.

Living with complexity is not an easy process. There are no simple answers or foolproof formulas for multifaceted problems. That is why radical thinkers include ideas from both one hand and the other. This can create a dynamic tension that transcends conventional thinking and moves toward revolutionary ideas. In fact, it's the very tension that drives the universe. Wisdom requires the ability to see the whole. A wise person is capable of finding harmony in contradiction, and resolving and embracing dichotomies.

If we are honest, most of our experiences include both good and bad times. Most people have both good traits and bad traits. Our lives will become bigger and healthier if we expand our thinking to include seemingly contradictory ideas, and move to the bigger life that God created for us.

In this book, there are fifty-two paradoxes divided into three categories: Mind, Body, and Spirit. Each paradox speaks to all three categories, but they are more appropriate for one. For example, the Mind chapters speak more to the habits of mental discipline.

The Body chapters speak to the importance of being aware of our actions. The Spirit chapters speak to moving away from fear and back to love.

The paradoxes are designed to invite you to ponder, contemplate, and integrate truth into your life on a daily basis. These weekly meditations are written with truths from different religions, traditions, and cultures. The reason for this non-dogmatic, eclectic, and inclusive approach is to help us see with new eyes the truths we have known for years. For example, Paradox Thirty-five states: "In giving you receive." The Christian scripture, "As you sow, so shall ye reap," is compatible with the Buddhist concept of karma. I share both religious precepts to challenge the reader to see how this truth—from the perspective of two different religions—helps us understand how we create our own heavenly and hellish experiences.

In each chapter, I offer seven concrete "Today, I will ...." statements for daily implementation of these paradoxical, abstract ideas. The seventh statement is left blank for you to add your specific, personal statement of truth and practice.

Janus is the Roman god who is depicted with two faces; one looking at what is behind and the other looking toward the future. Janus is the god of gates and doors, the guardian of exits and entrances. He presides over all that is double-edged in life and represented the transition between primitive and civilized, the countryside and the city, and peace and war. The ancient Romans thought what Janus stood for was so important that the first month of the year was named after him. Accepting the interplay and connectiveness between opposites is one of the important keys which will open new doors for you on your journey.

Carol Munson, writer and expert in the field of holistic healing said, "The universe is a big place, but that's okay—you'll grow into it." Learning about paradoxes and practicing "both-and" thinking will help your hero's journey in your big universe. Embracing paradoxes will help prepare you to face the inevitabilities of contradictions and to work constructively toward accommodation.

While reading these fifty-two paradoxes, stay with them by journaling, meditating, and processing them with others.   In time, you will see that paradoxes are common sense (this is a paradox). And this will catapult us on our journey and add sacredness to our ordinary experiences (another paradox). Indeed, *little you can live a big life*.

Chapter One
Mind-Body-Spirit

Simple isn't easy.

"It's simple, just trust in God."
"It's simple, just add and subtract and your checkbook will balance."
"It's simple, just eat less and you'll lose weight."

Simple is <u>not</u> easy! Just knowing this paradox can help you take the first step on a new adventure. Why? Because no one wants to look or feel dumb. Many "simple" projects or steps of faith are never started because people are afraid to fail at a "simple" thing.

The Eastern adage "The longest journey starts with a single step" is a good reflection for this paradox. A person can get paralyzed if he gets too tied up in the end result. The goal will seem too big or too overwhelming. If the goal is broken down into steps, the process will not seem so difficult.

Many New Year resolutions are discarded soon

after being made. Why? The "simple" goals of losing weight, exercising, quitting smoking, or reading more, are unrealistic expectations. Setting shorter-term and more modest goals or intentions creates more attainable successes and can start a positive momentum.

Woody Hayes, head football coach of Ohio State University for twenty-eight years, said, "There's nothing in this world that comes easy. There are a lot of people who aren't going to bother to win. We learn in football to get up and go once more." Perseverance is a necessary trait when the "simple" task or intention doesn't turn out to be "easy." Samuel Johnson one of eighteenth century England's best known literary figures, said, "Great works are performed not by strength, but by perseverance." Josh Billings, humorist and writer, said, "Be like a postage stamp—stick to one thing until you get there."

Something that might by easy becomes difficult when one does it reluctantly. Children show us this all the time. Simple requests like "take out the garbage," or "clean up your room," become incredibly difficult because of the child's reluctant attitude. Adults can learn from children and check their attitudes about exercising, or spending within their means, or other "simple" projects they've started but never finished.

People often "pick up a stick and beat themselves with it," if they do not accomplish what they think should be easy. This imaginary stick can be manifested in negative self-talk and unhealthy emotional baggage. Knowing that "simple isn't easy" allows them to be gentler on themselves.

The good news is we can get beyond being stuck and create a bigger life for ourselves. An ancient Buddhist proverb says, "If we are facing in the right direction, all we have to do is keep on walking." Not hastily or hurriedly, but by simply walking, putting one foot in front of another. British Reformed Baptist preacher, Charles Haddon Spurgeon said, "By perseverance the snail reached the Ark."

Writing this book on paradoxes was overwhelming. It seemed that writing on 52 paradoxes should be a *simple* task! After all, it was not a daily meditation book, which would require 365 passages. The writing process was not *easy* when quotes, stories, and parables for all fifty-two paradoxes had to be found. The commitment to write on just one paradox at a time was one of the necessary steps on the journey to completing this book.

While you are reading the following paradoxes, some of the truths might sound simple. For example, "letting go" (Paradox Thirty-six) might seem like a simple truth. Living "in each and every moment" (Paradox Nine) may appear simple to implement. If the process isn't that easy, be gentle with your self, smile, and keep practicing. Soon, you will find successes. You will find practices that make your life bigger. Truly, little you can live a big life!

Today, I will accept that simple is not easy by
_____.

Today, I will break a project down into steps so I can start the long journey by _____.

Today, I will let go of the "stick" that I have used to beat myself with and gently start over by _____.

Today, I will rejoice in a simple process by _____.

Today, I will start a project by doing one step of it by _____.

Today, I will love and accept myself in simple, easy, and difficult moments by _____.

Today, I will _____.

Chapter Two
Mind-Body-Spirit

We are perfectly human, which means we are humanly imperfect.

It is okay to make mistakes. It is okay to make a wrong decision. It is okay to feel sad, or angry, or hurt. IT IS OKAY TO BE HUMAN!

If we are afraid of getting hurt, we might not take a risk and love another person. If we are afraid of failure, we might not ever attempt a new project. If we are afraid of committing a sin, we might not even leave our house.

The original interpretation of the Greek word sin means "miss the mark." That's it. Nothing about being bad or going to hell. You just missed the mark. You were simply being human.

Shel Silverstein wrote a wonderful fairy tale for adults titled *The Missing Piece.* It is a story of a circle that was missing a piece. A large wedge had been cut out of it. The circle wanted to be perfect and fill the missing area. It traveled around the countryside looking for a replacement piece. Because of its imperfection, it could only move slowly. It moved in an unhurried manner, admired the flowers, chatted with worms, enjoyed the sunshine, and found lots of different, interesting pieces. But none of them fit. Finally it found a piece that fit perfectly. Since it was now a perfect circle, it could roll very fast. It rolled so fast it no longer noticed the flowers, the warm sun, or talked to the worms. When it realized how different its life had become, it stopped, left its new-found piece by the side of the road and rolled slowly away.

Giacomo Leopardi, a nineteenth century Italian poet wrote, "It's not our disadvantages or shortcomings that are ridiculous, but rather the studious way we try to hide them and our desire to act as if they did not exist." We are all going to miss the mark, we all have shortcomings—that is human. It is also human to learn our lessons, grow, develop, and mature. We humans have a self-actualizing drive that motivates us to practice with the hope of eventually hitting the mark.

In fifteenth century Japan, a counter-cultural movement against materialism and extravagance emerged. This movement was called wabi-sabi which is the art of finding imperfections and honoring authenticity. Leonard Koren states in his book, *Wabi-Sabi for Artists, Designers, Poets and Philosophers*, "… wabi-sabi appeared to be the perfect antidote to the pervasively slick, saccharine, corporate style of beauty that I felt was desensitizing American society." Some of the truths that wabi-sabi is based upon are (1) all things are impermanent; everything is changing and wearing down, (2) all things are imperfect. If you look more closely at things, you will see flaws. With impermanence, things are becoming "less perfect, more irregular and perhaps, more lovely." (3) All things are incomplete. Everything, including the universe itself, is in a constant state of evolving or dissolving.

If you recognize your own "wabi-sabi-ness," your own "Missing Piece," you will find a unique beauty and richness within yourself. If you find you made a faux pas in a social interaction, define the mistake and practice getting closer to the mark. If you see a blemish on your face, remember part of Lauren Hutton's beauty is the gap between her teeth. If you made a parenting mistake, name it, tame it, and then practice a new parenting style. *Our goal is not to become perfect, but to become more whole.* Within our imperfections, if we allow God to help us on our journey toward wholeness, we will live a bigger life.

Today, I will graciously accept the imperfections in my life. Specifically, the one I will name, tame, and change is _____.

Today, I will gently accept my humanness by _____.

Today, I will embrace my "Missing Piece" by _____.

Today, even though I will try not to make the same mistakes again, I will rejoice in my imperfect humanness by _____.

Today, I will recognize "wabi-sabi-ness" while growing toward my self-actualizing potential by _____.

Today, if I miss the mark, I will try again to get closer to the center of the target by _____.

Today, I will _____.

Chapter Three
Mind-Body-Spirit

Attitude is a little thing that makes a big difference.

During World War II, Jewish author Viktor Frankl chose to stay with his Austrian family despite holding a visa to flee to the United States. Of his family members, only he survived the concentration camps. He wrote about his experiences in *Man's Search for Meaning*: "Everything can be taken from a man but one thing: the last of human freedoms—to choose one's attitude in any given set of circumstances, to choose one's own way."

The children's story *The Little Engine That Could* speaks to this paradox wonderfully. The little train had to climb a big hill to deliver toys to the children of the next village. The mountain looked very steep and large in the eyes of the little train. But the little train knew how important it was to reach the village.

So the little train started and then kept saying to itself, "I think I can, I think I can," while climbing the hill. Because of this big attitude, the little train climbed the mountain, delivered the toys, and made all the children of the village happy.

The lesson of this story is attitude—in this case, determination. Attitude is one of many ingredients that determine success. But it is one of the most powerful ingredients; it is the yeast that makes the bread rise.

Scott Hamilton, the Olympic gold medal figure skater, retired because of cancer. He has been successfully treated, and it now skating and living well. Through this extremely difficult process he learned a very valuable lesson that he shares with audiences: "The only disability in life is a bad attitude."

There are many things we cannot change. We cannot change our past. We cannot change the fact that people will be rude to us. We cannot change the rain that pours on the weekend. The one thing we can change is our attitude about these things. We can change it because we initially created it. Many wise people know that life is ten percent what happens to us and ninety percent how we react to it. Abraham Lincoln said, "Most of us are about as happy as we make up our minds to be."

If your attitude is that you think you will not succeed at a specific endeavor, guess what? You probably won't succeed. If your attitude is positive, you will probably succeed. Dr. Norman Vincent Peale, minister and author of forty-six books said:

"Hold an image of the life you want, and that image will become fact."

When you are a leader, parent, friend, or co-worker, people take their cue from you on how to act and react. It you act like you're having a bad day, it is very difficult for those around you to act energetic and positive towards you. Be aware of your negative attitude, put aside your personal problems, and inspire others to join you in achieving bold goals.

Many people are stuck in an attitude of negativity and are trying just to survive and get through each day. A helpful strategy to rise above this is to create a gratitude journal. Writing every day about something for which you are grateful slowly creates a new attitude about life. Gratitude is an attitude! A reminder of this is my license plate: it reads B GR8FUL. Rabbi Mordecai Finley said as part of a presentation on Jewish spiritual practices, "There is no difference in happiness between rich and poor people. The deciding factor is gratefulness. Those who are grateful in their outlook are happiest."

Even if it is a cloudy day, you do not have to have a storm-cloud outlook. If your attitude in the morning is "it's going to be a great day," you will make it a great day. This little ritual in the morning will make a big difference in your day. It will make your life bigger.

Today, I will practice keeping a positive attitude by

_____.

Today, I will change my attitude about a task that has to be accomplished by _____.

Today, I will notice my attitude and try to change it to a more positive outlook by _____.

Today, I will be the Little Engine That Could by _____.

Today, I will practice being free of the disability of a bad attitude by _____.

Today, I will be aware of my thinking process—is it positive or negative by _____.

Today, I will _____.

Chapter Four
Mind-Body-Spirit

There is nothing permanent except change.

Change is one of the truths of life. Look around you. The seasons continually change. The sun was shining this morning, and tonight raindrops hit the windowpane. Our children become young adults. Our bodies are always shedding old cells and creating new ones. The people who cross our path are always changing. Our hair turns gray (or falls out). Technology is constantly changing.

The Buddha realized that change is one of the three characteristics of existence. He labeled this characteristic "impermanence"—everything is in a state of flux. He said that impermanence is not good or bad. It is just the way things are. Understanding and accepting impermanence leads to the avoidance of unrealistic expectations. For example, young children will excitedly run to the door when parents come home. But this heart-warming behavior will change when they get older. This is an opportunity to accept change and then greet them where they are in the house.

We know the dynamic of change to be true. We like change in the easy things: new books to read, new computer programs. Yet our egos do not like change. On a deeper level we crave stability. Our egos want to hold on to what they know. Sometimes we resist change and hold on to relationships, jobs, or attitudes that are not healthy for us. We are fearful of the unknown (changing jobs, finding new friends, etc.) and then rationalize not changing by saying, "Well, at least I know *this*. Change could bring something worse to me." Nobel Prize winning author John Steinbeck wrote about our human resistance to change, "It is the nature of man as he grows older to protest against change, particularly change for the better."

Change frightens us the most when we are placing our faith in earthly things—people, institutions, churches, or situations. We more naturally embrace change when we are placing our faith in God. It is a prayerful practice to lean upon God's infinite understanding rather than our own finite way of seeing things.

Water is a good example of how to accept change. When water runs into a rock in the river, it doesn't curse at the rock and fight that impediment. The water naturally flows around it. Why doesn't a river run perfectly straight? When the water reaches an obstacle, rather than resisting, it changes course.

Even when the temperature gets too hot, water doesn't oppose and defy, but changes into steam. The lesson is to be like water and go with the flow.

Being open to change and allowing the natural changes to occur in our lives can be very freeing. This is not always easy. But ultimately there is nothing we can hold on to or keep forever—except our own souls. (And even these belong to God.)

Leo Buscaglia, Ph.D., a renowned lecturer, author, and University of Southern California professor who was famous for his "Love Class" said: "An investment in life is an investment in change…you've got to continue to keep adjusting to change, which means that you are going to be facing new obstacles. That's the joy of living. And once you are in the process of becoming, there is no stopping."

A friend has this simple, three-line message on her refrigerator:

Life is change.
Growth is optional.
Choose wisely.

Don't just expect change; prepare for it and embrace it. This practice will create a bigger life—one you were created to live.

Today, I will be open to the truth of change by
_____.

Today, I will not fight the natural changes that are occurring in my life. Specifically, I will
_____.

Today, I will embrace impermanence by _____.

Today, I will make an incremental step toward a healthier behavior by _____.

Today, I will react gently when an unforeseen change happens in my life by _____.

Today, I will be like water and go with the flow by _____.

Today, I will _____.

Chapter Five
Mind-Body-Spirit

The journey forward is the journey inward.

A student asked his master if he needed to embrace some spiritual path to be healed. The master smiled, leaned forward, pointed directly to his heart, and whispered, "You are the path." Recognizing that there was nowhere to go but in, that he was the path and that he had to tread himself wholeheartedly, he found his questions were answered.

Western culture teaches us that moving forward in life is done by accumulating external things like prestige, wealth, and material goods. It is a common belief that forward movement includes securing job promotions, working long hours, and earning bigger paychecks. This philosophy tends to create empty lives and middle age crises. Mythologist Joseph Campbell told the story of the person who spent his whole life climbing the corporate ladder only to find at the end it was leaning against the wrong building. Campbell further stated, "Follow your bliss and doors will open where there were no doors before."

The true journey forward is only found by looking inward to your self. One can move forward and more easily find God's will by resolving old anger or grief issues. Looking inward to figure out why a certain person can push your buttons allows you to take ownership of the problem, which will create healing and help break your unhealthy cycles of living. Buddha said, "Through awareness and perseverance you can break this cycle of birth and death and find yourself elevated to the highest. Therefore, awareness leads you forward, while lack of awareness leads you nowhere."

Taking ownership of "negative" feelings is a difficult process. It is much easier to blame something external. An interesting way of looking at this truth is by this metaphor: If you squeeze a lemon, what comes out of it is lemon juice because that's what is inside—that's what a lemon is. When someone squeezes you, the same applies. If out of you comes anger, hatred, jealousy or fear, it isn't because of who did the squeezing; it isn't because of the circumstances; it is because that is what is inside of you. What's inside of you is there because of how your life experiences and how you choose to think about and process your life.

Feelings are messengers. If someone makes you angry, you need to look inward and ask yourself, "What is the message from that feeling?" Is the feeling triggering old control or abandonment issues from a parent? Is the feeling telling you this person is toxic and you need to limit your time with him? Are you in a one sided conversation, feeling frustrated because you realize you are just waiting for your turn to talk? The journey forward is not to blame the other person for your anger. It is looking inward to the message from your specific feeling.

If a person attempts to build intimacy with another before the work of looking inward and becoming a whole and healthy person is done, the relationship will be an attempt to fill the hole inside. Every relationship will be an attempt to get something to make you feel okay. Ralph Waldo Emerson addressed this dis-ease when he wrote, "Nothing can bring you peace, but yourself."

Jesus taught us that the kingdom of God is within. Joseph Campbell wrote, "It is within you that the Divine lives." God resides inside each and every one of us. The soulful journey forward takes place when we travel inside ourselves and find the strength, wisdom and courage to travel home—to our true self.

If other people are not on the same sacred journey, they might not honor your true self. If they are following a path more revered by culture, they might become uncomfortable with your honest journey. In 1854, Henry David Thoreau penned, "If a man does not keep pace with his companions, perhaps it is because he hears a different drummer. Let him step to the music he hears, however measured or far away."

It takes strength and perseverance to honor our uniqueness. And, as Robert Frost so beautifully penned: "I took the road less traveled by, and that has made all the difference." The difference will be a bigger life.

Today, I will not blame others. I will look inward to resolve the problem by _____.

Today, I will see what it is about me that cause my anger or anxiety by _____.

Today, I will embrace the kingdom of God, which is inside of me by _____.

Today, I will name the "hole that is inside my heart" and start the healing process by _____.

Today, I will change myself, which will change my world by _____.

Today, I will spend time in meditation so I can truly listen to my inner world by _____.

Today, I will _____.

Chapter Six
Mind-Body-Spirit

Some people never go crazy, and lead insane lives.

Many follow the conventional "truths" of the world. The "truths" are broad and cover all areas of our lives: "men should ....," "women should ....," "money will ....," "my life partner should ....." Whether these admonitions are learned from parents, friends, or culture, they create the same reality: life inside a small box.

It is hard to see outside the box and live a bigger life when you are inside of it. This creates a sense of unknowing, which is uncomfortable. People then tend to look for affirmation for their lifestyle of working long hours, hoarding their resources, and/or talking about others. They receive support from their friends, family members, television, and co-workers, which perpetuates this insane cycle.

At a deeper level within ourselves, we desire the freedom of living a bigger life outside the box. This inner wisdom might seem crazy to the more cultured outside world. We move from small steps like playing in the rain and jumping in puddles, to bigger steps of leaving a lucrative but deadening job. These acts of "craziness" can bring more joy and peace to our lives. American pilot Charles Lindbergh said, "Real freedom lies in wildness, not in civilization."

The "what ifs" and "I shoulds" keep us in our daily ruts. *"What if* the new venture I start fails?" *"What if* the economy takes a downturn?" *"I should* stay in this job because I've already put in ten years." *"What if* I start living my faith more fully—will people think I'm weird?" All these questions and statements keep us in our small, insane, and unhappy lives.

It is insane to live by other people's norms. Most of us are taught to "color inside the lines," "don't make waves," and "be a nice girl/good boy." If we are not ever told to "find your voice," "follow your bliss," or it's okay to "walk to the beat of a different drummer," our lives will become insanely small. Author and professor of Early American History at Harvard University, Laurel Thatcher Ulrich, said, "Well behaved women rarely make history."

Cultural norms help maintain order in a complex society. To a large degree, that is helpful. The problem occurs when we adopt these norms hook, line, and sinker. We then live our lives in a socially programmed hypnosis. We collectively agree to live these fictions. Most people never see them as false, because everyone else is doing them! For example, western culture encourages people to keep busy. We get complimented for multi-tasking. We get our kids involved in many after-school and summer activities. When we see someone and politely ask, "How are you?", a common response is "busy." The first person will then respond, "I'm busy too." And the treadmill gets walked on again and goes round and round. Gandhi said, "There is more to life than increasing its speed." Some people exit the rat race; and they tend to be the happiest people.

It definitely feels like a risk to go against the norm. Sue Monk Kidd writes in her book *When the Heart Waits*, "Now and then, in search of your True Self, you have to find the courage to enter a great absurdity. Kierkegaard pointed out that courage isn't the absence of despair and fear but the capacity to move ahead in spite of them."

In medieval times, the court jester was often the king's best advisor. By playing the fool, he exposed the conventional truths which made the kingdom dysfunctional. The court jester's "craziness" helped stop the insanity.

Blessed are the cracked—for they shall see the light! That light will lead people to freedom and a bigger life.

Today, I will get a little bit crazy by _____.
Today, I will let go of "what if" thinking by _____.
Today, I will venture outside my box by _____.
Today, I will let go of one "I should" by _____.
Today, I will listen to the court jester by _____.

Today, I will name a cultural "truth" that does not fit with my own inner truth by _____.

Today, I will _____.

Chapter Seven
Mind-Body-Spirit

The teacher learns the most.

A friend recently agreed to give a presentation on a subject that was outside her area of expertise. She spent countless hours reading, researching, and writing about the topic. On the day of the seminar, she gave an outstanding speech. Before ending, she thanked the organization for asking her to present. She said, "I agreed to give this lecture because I wanted to gain more knowledge about this area. I hope you learned something too; but by analyzing the current research, reading many different perspectives, and synthesizing the material, I know I have learned the most."

Parents are teachers of children. Young children can ask the most simple and profound questions. For example, "Mommy, what does love mean?" "Daddy, how do you forgive a person?" "Mommy, what happens after you die?" It is sometimes hard to put words to concepts like death, love, and forgiveness. To fully honor the child's question, and then answer it, takes some deep and quick thinking. By teaching the child the meaning of these words and concepts, the parent learns more fully about these truths of life.

Aristotle said, "Teaching is the highest form of understanding." Many professors know this so they utilize the teaching technique of having their students teach some of the material. The process of making a presentation forces the student to understand the material so he or she can talk intelligently about it. Opening yourself up to being a teacher will increase your own learning. If you want to grow, expand, and stretch yourself, then agree to teach a Sunday school class, or a Scout troop, or a seminar at your workplace. You will be surprised at how much you learn and now much bigger your life becomes.

Seneca, the Roman philosopher, playwright, and tutor to young Nero said, "Men learn while they teach." French essayist Joseph Joubert wrote, "To teach is to learn twice." These two quotes, written from different eras and from different countries, speak to the truth that preparing to instruct others is the best way to instruct oneself.

Charles Schulz, the creator of the "Peanuts" cartoon said, "Life is like a ten-speed bicycle. Most of us have gears we never use." This happens because we allow our lives to become very narrow and small. Most of us use the excuse that there is not enough time for anything besides work and family. If we are truly motivated to learn or do something new, we must make time. We can set better boundaries at work, use our commute time better, not watch as much television, or divide and conquer the parenting responsibilities. When you make your life a little bit bigger, remember to pass on your new knowledge. This will continue to make your life bigger.

The Chinese proverb, "Learning is a treasure that will follow its owner everywhere," speaks to the benefit of being a life-long learner. Physically, if our muscles are stretched, they will grow bigger and stronger. Similarly, our minds need to be stretched and old ideas torn apart. When we practice working our minds, we will be sharper and more astute. Then, when we join in any conversation, we will pass on our new ideas, which will help us hone our thinking skills, and hopefully help someone else.

Chinese philosopher Confucius said, "I hear and I forget. I see and I remember. I do and I understand." The student "hears" and "sees," which allows a certain level of learning. The "doing" of the teacher integrates the information into understanding—which is a much deeper level. This will lead to living a bigger life.

Today, I will take time to more fully answer one of my children's questions by _____.

Today, I will begin an exercise program so I can then teach my children the importance and benefits of regular exercise by _____.

Today, I will write a guest editorial for the newspaper by _____.

Today, I will ask if a local club needs another volunteer by _____.

Today, I will ask if I can lead an adult education class at my church or synagogue by _____.

Today, I will ask if the English Language Learner classes in my local school need another volunteer by _____.

Today, I will _____.

Chapter Eight
Mind-Body-Spirit

To see truth, contemplate all phenomena as a lie.

The world is flat. The earth is the center of the universe. Separate but equal. The four-minute mile is unreachable. These were all "truths" at one time. People led their lives and were directly influenced by these perspectives. Inevitably, these "truths" led humanity to dead ends, small lives, and unhealthy behaviors.

Today, we are thankful for Columbus, Copernicus, Brown vs. Board of Education, and Roger Bannister for showing us these were lies. Their vision, insight, determination, and risk-taking have helped all of us to see life more clearly, honestly, and without such restricting boundaries.

Individually, we also need to look at life, specifically our own life, and see what "lies" are guiding us. Do I have to stay in a chaotic relationship? Do I have to work such long hours? Is my net-worth equal to my self-worth? Does my main parenting style have to be one that is constantly nagging? Do I have to please everyone?

The Buddha gave a sermon where he made a challenge to question the cultural norms. He said, "Do not believe in something solely because someone has told you so, or tradition has it, or because many others do. Test for yourself, experience for yourself." Following your heart and breaking free of what everyone else is doing can be lonely. The Buddha knew this and wrote, "Foolish people who know no better will laugh at those on a spiritual path. Take no notice, for their life is full of suffering."

Many of Jesus' actions and the parables he told were to challenge the rules and "truths" that governed the people. Jesus spoke to a Samaritan woman at the well that challenged the current day thinking that a Jew was better than a Samaritan. Jesus' actions showed that the gospel was good news for everyone...not just the Jews. Jesus turned over the money-changer tables in the synagogue because he wanted to discredit the "truth" that commerce was so important that it could transpire in holy places. Jesus forgave an adulterer when the people wanted to stone her.

Contemplate all phenomena in your life as a lie. Ask questions. Seek counseling. Talk to a minister, rabbi, or priest. Read books. Talk to a friend who you believe leads a healthy lifestyle. Hear the truths of a comedian. (Lily Tomlin said, "The trouble with being in the rat race is that even when you win you are still a rat.") Practicing these strategies will lead you to a more truthful and healthy existence. You will live a bigger life that is full of endless possibilities and choices.

There is a parable that says if you put a frog into a pot of boiling water it will leap out right away to escape danger. But if you put a frog in a pot of cool water, and then gradually heat the water until it starts boiling, the frog will not become aware of the threat until it's too late. Cultural influences can be like the cool water that is slowly heated to dangerous levels. For example, what is your definition of success? Most people state that success is being busy, making lots of money, owning expensive houses and cars, and being in the popular crowd. This "truth" can lead to a small, unhappy life where one is always striving for more wealth and continually being discontented. We need to define success for ourselves. Success could include being a great parent, volunteering at a local non-profit, or pursuing a hobby. Being busy has become a badge of honor which can slowly burn out a person—boil a person—to a slow death.

Most people do not want us to rock the boat of cultural truths. But if you want to walk on water, you have to get out of the boat. French author and winner of the Nobel Prize in literature in 1947, Andre Gide wrote, "One doesn't discover new lands without consenting to lose sight of shore for a very long time." Creating new truths is losing sight of what we know. To live a bigger life, we have to let go of our shorelines and sail out to new horizons.

Today, I will sit quietly and ponder what area of my life that needs to become healthier. Specifically, I will _____.

Today, I will contemplate on the idea that my thoughts and beliefs might be lies. Specifically, I will _____.

Today, I will talk to someone about how they see this phenomenon in life. Specifically, I will _____.

Today, I will take a risk and try a new worldview. Specifically, I will _____.

Today, I will try to erase an old mental tape created when someone told me I couldn't accomplish something I wanted to do. Specifically, I will ___ _____.

Today, I will change an old, unhealthy behavior. Specifically, I will _____.

Today, I will _____.

Chapter Nine
Mind-Body-Spirit

It is possible to live happily ever after if you live in each and every moment.

Cinderella lived happily ever after. As did Snow White and Rapunzel. Why isn't that happening to me?

These fairy tales sold us a bill of goods. The truths that they espoused are (1) someone else can save you, and (2) life can be easy, happy, and conflict free. In real life, no one else can do our healing and growing except ourselves. And only by "slaying the dragons" in our own life can we find freedom and joy.

Wouldn't it be nice if we were read fairy tales that told stories of living in the present moment? If the hero or heroine started thinking and living in the past or the future, he or she would temporarily lose his/her kingdom. At the end of the story, we would be told that the moral of these tales was "the present is a present," or "carpe diem" (seize the day), or even "be here now." These truths would help us live more fully and find joy in each successive moment. There would be a happily ever after...one moment at a time.

There are only three places our mind can take us: the past, present or future. Many of us live in the past, re-living hurtful experiences or re-living glory days of old. The problem with this lifestyle is you are living in an illusionary world. The past is gone with all of its hurt or fame. You are not living in reality! Living in the future can create worries and false stresses. These are also illusions. They feel real only because your mind is manufacturing them. Quit living in the past or future—they are distractions to peace and happiness. We can learn from the past and we can plan for the future—*and* we need to come back to the present for the place of our existence.

Eckhart Tolle writes in *The Power of Now,* that we have to use time in the practical aspects of our lives—which he calls "clock time." This includes planning our day, arriving at appointments on time, and learning from the past so we can continue to evolve. Tolle writes there is also "psychological time" which takes us out of the present moment in a dysfunctional manner. The narcissistic ego resides here and wants to sustain its victimized or glorified self of the past, or predict the future pains or pleasures, by creating and living in psychological time. This kind of thinking will create pain and give you a false sense of pleasure that, paradoxically, will turn into pain.

God said, "I am." We should strive to live where God is; in the present. The past is a thief that takes us away from the wonders of the present. The future is a false prophet that promises what it cannot deliver. The present is real. God resides there.

The Buddha said, "Our minds are too busy chasing after yesterday's memories or tomorrow's dreams. The only way to be in touch with life is to return to the present moment. Once you know how to return to the present moment, you will become awakened, and at that moment, you will find your true self." Sadly, most people are afraid of change and practice risk avoidance as a guiding principle. They never truly experience the present moment...so they never live happily ever after.

The present moment is brief and huge. This is where the big life resides.

Today, I will practice living in the moment by _____.
Today, I will create a new fairy tale for my life by
_____.
Today, I will let go of the past by _____.
Today, I will try to quit worrying about the future by
_____.
Today, I will create a better here and now by
_____.
Today, I will notice when I think in psychological time
and gently come back to the present moment by
_____.
Today, I will _____.

Chapter Ten
Mind-Body-Spirit

Get serious about a sense of humor.

Many people take life, themselves, and others way too seriously. Anger, resentment, frustration, jealousy, and even hatred occur because of a perspective of life that doesn't include a sense of humor.

Road rage is a good example. Our streets, highways, and interstates are busier than ever. When traffic moves "too slowly," people maneuver their cars so as to get to their destinations as soon as possible. The other day, I switched lanes and the person in the car behind me made an obscene gesture. Obviously he was irate. I internally checked my behavior. I had signaled, and there was plenty of room to change lanes. I knew I had not cut him off. This driver's reaction to me was absurd—so absurd that I found it humorous. I smiled to myself. In fact, even chuckled, and sent a prayer his way. I was reminded of a Mark Twain quote: "Humor is mankind's greatest blessing."

In the book *Way of the Peaceful Warrior*, Dan Millman meets a wise old man whom he nicknames Socrates. Socrates teaches Dan the path of spiritual awakening. After one of Socrates' early teachings, Dan felt he had "learned it all" and told Socrates that he no longer needed him as a mentor. Socrates burst out laughing and gave Dan a small card with embossed letters. It read:

Warrior Inc.,
Socrates, Prop.
Specializing in:
Paradox, Humor and Change.

Millman, like most of us, needed to more fully learn these three truths of life. The first truth, paradox, is what this book is about. The truth of change is described earlier in Paradox Four. In this chapter, humor is investigated.

Every one of us experiences difficulties at home and work. There are abundant problems in the community, country, and world. We need to genuinely work to improve situations *and* find humor along the way. Comedian Bill Cosby said, "Through humor, you can soften some of the worst blows that life delivers. And once you find laughter, no matter how painful your situation might be, you can survive it." Nineteenth century Congregational minister Henry Ward Beecher said, "A person without a sense of humor is like a wagon without springs. It's jolted by every pebble on the road."

Norman Cousins, former editor of *Saturday Review* was afflicted with coronary heart disease. Even though he received the best medical attention, he suffered a heart attack. After being stabilized in the hospital, one of the doctors told Cousins that he had to settle down and do nothing—which included no laughing. Soon after, Cousins heard a funny story and roared with laughter. He realized the laughter did not hurt him. In fact, he felt warm and relaxed. Cousins researched the power of laughter and humor. He reviewed the articles written by Dr. William F. Fry, Jr. of the Stanford School of Medicine in which Fry details the physiological benefits of laughter.

> Even if laughter produces no specific biochemical changes, it accomplishes one very essential purpose. It tends to block deep feelings of apprehension and even panic that all too frequently accompany serious illness. It helps free the body of the constricting effects of the negative emotions that in turn may impair the healing system.

Humor can be a life or death matter. We had better get serious about our sense of humor, in order to live a big life.

Today, I will laugh a little bit more.
Today, I will send a joke, cartoon, or funny story to a friend.
Today, I will buy a greeting card that makes me laugh out loud.
Today, I will find humor in an absurd situation.

Today, I will smile at a stranger.
Today, I will let out a belly laugh.
Today, I will _____.

Chapter Eleven
Mind-Body-Spirit

Males have feminine energy. Females have masculine energy.

A Native American saying is "Within every man there is a reflection of a woman, and within every woman there is a reflection of a man."

The psychologies of men and women are different and interrelated. But men are used to seeing themselves as only men, and women think of themselves as only women. The psychological facts show that every human being is androgynous.

The word androgynous includes two Greek words. *Andros* means man, and *gynos* means woman. These traits have nothing to do with our sexuality. They are core personality traits of each human being.

The Chinese knew this fact 4,000 years ago when they created the Yin-Yang symbol. This circle with a curved line in the middle, symbolizes the masculine and feminine energies in every human. Masculine energy is more rational, linear, objective, assertive, and movement is outward. Feminine energy is more open, receptive, cyclical, nurturing, synthesizing, and movement is more inward. Masculine energy is the "do" of life. Feminine energy is the "be" of life. Is one side better than the other? Of course not. There are benefits to having and utilizing each side. For example, without a relationship with the inner Yin, a man can focus but lacks emotion. He can strive for power, but he is unable to be creative because he cannot produce new life out of himself. And the opposite is true for a woman. If she is unable to assert and move out with her creative spirit, she will be powerless with her ideas. Only by the fruitful joining of the two energies can the soul become fully alive, and prevent life from becoming sterile.

If we allow ourselves to learn about our opposite side, growth and a more balanced lifestyle will occur. Our communication styles, relationships, and work efforts will be more functional and healthier. (*Men are from Mars, Women are from Venus* and *You Just Don't Understand Me* speaks to these issues.) We will also be happier because we have found our whole self.

Masculine and feminine energies are two sides of dualism. When we think of these energies in an "either-or" mentality, we live in a more limited manner which restricts our freedom. Many characters in literature, movies, and television are one-sided to create comic stereotypes. In the 1970's many families tuned in to *All in the Family* to laugh at the characters of Archie and Edith Bunker. Their narrow personalities created problems within themselves and their relationships.

Thinking of these energies in a "both-and" mentality, allows a dynamic interaction between these traits. A more balanced, mature person evolves who can live a life of more possibilities.

We call our planet "mother earth" because plants, vegetables, and fruits are born from the fertile soil. But for new growth to appear, the complement of "father sky" needs to provide the rain, light, and warmth. Only by coupling these two energies does the system work.

Sometimes we limit God by only using masculine pronouns and nouns. The Divine power is not only assertive, strong, and self-confident, as a father would be, but also loving, nurturing, and caring, as a mother would be. The Hebrew word "Jehovah" is both masculine and feminine. By viewing our Higher Being with both energies, we will not limit our God which would limit our relationship with the Divine.

We are made in the image of God. By embracing our masculine and feminine energies, we will more likely live to our full potential. Little you will live a bigger life.

Today, I will practice one personality trait from the other side by _____.

Today, I will find a healthy person of the opposite sex who can help me learn more about their psychological traits by _____.

Today, I will read a book on the different ways men and women see the world by _____.

Today, I will try to be more androgynous by _____.

Today, I will be open to the fullness of my Higher Being by _____.

Today, I will practice a balance between the masculine "do" and the feminine "be" by _____.

Today, I will _____.

Chapter Twelve
Mind-Body-Spirit

Playing it safe is the most dangerous thing you could do.

This paradoxical truth is very easy to see in the raising of children. At the correct developmental time period, parents do not allow their children the safe position of staying in diapers. Instead, parents challenge the toddlers to use the toilet. Parents also challenge their toddlers to verbalize their thoughts and transition from the safety of crawling to walking. Many five and six year olds across the country want to remain in the safety of their homes, but parents lead them by the hand into kindergarten classes.

Football and basketball coaches mentally and physically push their athletes to hone their skills and play better. Sometimes they forget this and lose games because they sit on leads and have their players play too conservatively. As adults, we do not have parents or coaches pushing and leading us to grow into new frontiers. Because of this, we tend to do what children want to do—stay in our safety zones.

Two important questions we need to ask ourselves are: (1) Where am I playing it too safe? and, (2) Why am I staying in this dangerously safe situation?

Are you playing it too safe in a job you outgrew years ago? Is it in friendships that are stale? Is it in the quality of your marriage where conflicts are more common then intimacy?

In the 1987 movie *Moonstruck*, Loretta, played by Cher, is in her late 30's and single. She is tired of looking for true love so she conveniently gets engaged to a neighborhood friend. He leaves to visit his dying mother in Sicily, and Loretta meets Ronny, her fiancé's younger brother, played by Nicolas Cage. Ronny falls in love with Loretta. She fights her feelings of love for Ronny, for the obvious reason of being engaged to his brother. Ronny tries many ways to win Loretta's heart. He's finally successful when he tells her this paradoxical truth about the danger of playing life too safe.

The journey of personal and spiritual growth includes many periods of unknowing and uncertainty. Times of not feeling emotionally safe are normal when one is growing and evolving. This goes against one's ego, which always wants the safe status quo.

Our soul wants us to grow to our full potential in all areas of our lives. Staying with the status quo is the opposite of this innate drive to wholeness. For example, the acorn might want to live in the safety of the soil. But it pushes itself up toward the light to become the mighty oak tree because that is the way it was created. Fear is the dynamic that keeps us "playing it safe" (Chapter Forty-seven). Self-help author Brian Tracy wrote, "It is not failure itself that holds you back; it is the fear of failure that paralyzes you." Motivational speaker and author Les Brown said, "Too many of us are not living our dreams because we are living our fear."

We are designed to grow and venture onto the seas of life. We have been given free will yet many people choose to stay stagnant. We have a choice to stay safe or push ourselves to our full potential. Horace Mann, nineteenth century educational reformer wrote, "Be ashamed to die until you have won some victory for humanity." When we dare to live fully, we will create positive direction that will, by definition, help others.

A boat that is tied to the dock is very safe—but it is not serving its designed purpose—and it is going nowhere. Living life dangerously does not necessarily mean taking wild risks. Living dangerously is not taking any risks.

Irish playwright and essayist George Bernard Shaw wrote, "I want to be all used up when I die." Having a small life is stifling. Extend yourself, untie the knot that is keeping you trapped and stuck and take a calculated risk. Continue to share your gifts and talents. There is a bigger life out there for you.

Today, I will name a way I am living too safely by
_____.

Today, I will take a small risk and move out of a dangerously safe position by _____.

Today, I will not accept the status quo in my life by _____.

Today, I will "parent" myself and give effort to live more toward my fullpotential by _____.

Today, I will use the acorn as an inspiration and start my growth to the light by _____.

Today, I will journal on dangerous safety by _____.

Today, I will _____.

Chapter Thirteen
Mind-Body-Spirit

By not making a decision, you are making
a decision.

An adult was in counseling because he was very unhappy with his job. He felt stuck, underappreciated, and depressed. The workplace was definitely unhealthy for him. Week after week he bemoaned his existence at work. He couldn't understand how his boss picked on him but allowed other employees to do the same thing. He would share that on Sunday nights a dark cloud would enter his house because he knew work was the next morning.

Nonetheless, he continued to stay at a job that was toxic. During one of the counseling sessions, he was asked, "Do you realize that by not making a decision, you are making a decision to stay?" He responded with a surprised look, and then the light bulb went on for him.

Helping him required many exercises to free him so he could make a move to a new profession. He had seen himself a victim of his boss, fellow employees, and the overall workplace. With this new insight that his inertia was a decision to stay, he realized that he was in control of his own destiny. He now could make a conscious decision to not be a victim and start looking for a new job.

Parents empower their children to make good choices. We start at an early age to teach them how to make decisions. For example, parents will ask at bedtime, "Do you want to walk to your room or do you want me to carry you?" We remind them during adolescence to make safe choices when they go out with friends. Sometimes as adults, we forget that we always have choices. The circumstances do not always include easy decisions…but we always have choices.

The tough choices of life do not have to be made alone. There are many support systems that help people through their difficult decisions. There are churches, synagogues, and mosques that have helped people through the ages. There are professionals who are trained and objective and can see the "forest from the trees." There are good friends who can "lend an ear." John Donne wrote, "No man is an island entire of itself, every man is a piece of the continent." This famous quote reminds us to not separate our self from community. We need to find healthy people who can support and help us make choices that will take us from a toxic environment to a more tonic one.

If you feel that somewhere in your life you are

stuck, realize that you are not alone and, with the help of a trusted friend or professional, you may create movement toward a new decision.

Fear of failure is a big dynamic that can keep one stuck in life. Truman Capote said, "Failure is the condiment that gives success its flavor." When you eat a wonderful meal, Capote is saying that failure is not the main course. It plays a small role, like salt, ketchup, or oregano. No one says "The pepper really made this meal," because it is only a little spice that enhances the main dish. Similarly, you may taste some failure along your life path. But by making good, solid decisions to move in a direction that you know is right, the end result will be delectable and scrumptious.

Mahatma Gandhi said, "You may never know what results come of your action, but if you do nothing there will be no result." By including grounded people in your life, acknowledging fear yet trusting your Higher Power and yourself, and taking calculated risks, you will make decisions that will create a bigger life for yourself.

Today, I will name an area in my life where I am stuck by _____.

Today, I will realize an area in my life where I am choosing to not make a decision as my decision by _____.

Today, I will talk to someone who will help me see the forest from the trees by _____.

Today, I will start looking at options that will help me get unstuck by _____.

Today, I will actually make a decision that will start the movement toward something healthier by _____.

Today, I will stop seeing myself as a victim, and start creating a new destiny for myself by _____.

Today, I will _____.

Chapter Fourteen
Mind-Body-Spirit

What we learn from the past is that we seldom learn from the past.

In high school an excellent teacher of Greco-Roman history gave bonus points to those students who recognized a civilization that learned from the past. The reason this merited extra credit points was because there are few examples and she wanted her students to realize this.

We humans seldom learn from our past. We repeat negative patterns inherited from our parents and their parents. We repeat unhealthy patterns from our culture, and we repeat self-defeating patterns that we personally have created over the years. We frequently fall into ruts.

Adults who were raised by an alcoholic parent are often married to an alcoholic. Adults who were raised by a workaholic parent often experience a marriage crisis because of work issues.

Spanish born American philosopher George Santayana's statement succinctly states this paradox: "Those who cannot remember the past are condemned to repeat it." For example, countless writers from different cultures have acknowledged that money can't buy happiness. But most of us continue to pursue the mythological American dream and tie our self-worth to our net-worth. Another example is parents with older children tell parents with younger children that children grow up very fast, so embrace each and every day with them. But many parents busy themselves with work and activities and miss important childhood experiences. Jesus, Gandhi, Martin Luther King, Jr., and countless others taught us to "love your neighbor" and to live in non-violent ways. But centuries pass, wars continue, and our culture is more litigious than ever.

Not learning from the past creates a present-day prison. Our tendency is to blame our parents, ex-partner, or culture. But it is our own beliefs and ideas that imprison us. We rarely ask ourselves why a negative pattern continues. Albert Einstein said, "Learn from yesterday, live for today, hope for tomorrow. The important thing is not to stop questioning." If we don't look at ourselves, we will unconsciously act out the self-defeating behaviors. This creates a negative ripple effect for future generations and ourselves.

Breaking old behavior patterns can be difficult. The first step is to be aware of a negative pattern that is being repeated in your life. The next step is to name the new behavior that you want to create. Then practice, practice, and practice the new way of living. You learned the old behavior. Now you are going to learn a new behavior. You can even "fake it until you make it." The point is to not blame, but to take responsibility and move on from the past...so you will earn extra credit points in the classroom called life.

Oscar Wilde, Irish poet and novelist, wrote "Be yourself, everyone else is already taken." This witty comment reminds us that we do not need to live out the messages we learned from a parent, sibling, or culture. We can learn from their mistakes, and integrate a new way of living in the world. American Bishop Thomas S. Monson wrote, "The past is behind, learn from it. The future is ahead, prepare for it. The present is here, live it."

Mark Twain penned, "History is a gallery of pictures in which there are few originals and many copies." The originals are examples of healthy and unhealthy ways of living in the world. Which ones are you going to copy? If we learn from the past—and learn from healthy "copies"—we will have much bigger lives in the present.

Today, I am going to name an unhealthy behavior that I see being repeated in my life. Specifically, I will _____.

Today, I am going to name a new, healthier behavior that I would like to practice. Specifically, I will _____.

Today, I am going to practice, practice, and practice again, the new, healthier behavior by _____.

Today, I am going to be a student of my life and discern if I am repeating negative patterns from my family's history. I will _____.

Today, I am going to gain "extra credit" in life and learn from my past. Specifically, I will _____-

Today, since "everyone else is taken," I will be myself by _____.

Today, I am going to _____.

Chapter Fifteen
Mind-Body-Spirit

"Unnatural thinking feels natural to us,
and natural thinking feels unnatural."
Marianne Williamson

A *Course in Miracles* teaches that there are only two ways of living in the world: from a state of love or fear. This philosophy says that we are born perfectly in a state of love—which is the true and natural state of our being.

Most of us learn both of these states from our parents and culture. But slowly and insidiously we are programmed to think in more fearful ways, and the world then becomes unsafe and unfriendly. For example, we are taught to look out only for number one. We are told that accumulation of wealth is very important, and we are more valuable if we dress, look and act in certain ways. Our ego then develops to think in fearful and unnatural ways. Greed, selfishness, anger, and separateness become common reactions to life. We become non-accepting and aversive to many circumstances that cross our path. Desire and cravings become commonplace because we think pleasurable experiences (trips, sex, food) and material goods will fill the voids of our life. Because of our "unnatural thinking," we are forever trying to control life. Life is a struggle.

Peace, joy, compassion, forgiveness, connectiveness, acceptance, and being non-judgmental are natural expressions of love. These are gifts from the Spirit and our original, natural state of existence. Yet these natural thoughts start to feel unnatural when we practice fearful ways of thinking. These states might sound wonderful during Sunday morning church service, or appropriate for Jesus, Buddha, Gandhi, and others, but not for our day-to-day grind.

We look around us and see the practices of the dominant culture: galloping consumerism, individualism, narrowly defined patriotism, and an ethical standard that lands people in jail. We might want our lifestyle to express more of the Spirit's movement, and less of the spirit of the times, but there are few models to follow. When we practice nonviolence in our thoughts and actions, who can we talk to about our experiences? Are places of worship challenging us to transcend these unnatural thoughts?

The difficult truth of this paradox is tied into Paradox Thirty-five—"In giving you receive." If you live out fearful expressions of greed, hostility, or being non-trusting, you will receive these in return. This creates a negative self-fulfilling prophecy.

Albert Einstein said, "The most beautiful thing we can experience is the mysterious. It is the source of all true art and science." There is mystery in the power of love, forgiveness, compassion, and realizing everything is inner-connected. Paradoxes are mysterious. We are pulled toward these truths and ways of living. The reason they resonate is because like attracts like. At our core, we are love. We are attracted to all the beautiful things that are manifested from love.

In the Biblical scripture of Matthew 7:24-27, Jesus tells us that we must build our house on rock, not sand. This parable is telling us that we need to train our thinking process back to its natural state. Start perceiving the world from a rock-solid position of love. Ask your minister, priest, or rabbi for guidance, for a fellowship group to join, and books to read. Ask for a miracle and start the journey back home to a bigger life.

Today, I will start to replace fearful thoughts with loving thoughts.
Today, I will create a loving, self-fulfilling prophecy.
Today, I will embrace and integrate a loving act from a scripture in my Holy Books.
Today, I will start the process of building my "house of thoughts" on a solid foundation.
Today, I will start the process of seeing that all my thoughts originate either from love or fear.
Today, I will return to my original state of love.
Today, I will _____.

Chapter Sixteen
Mind-Body-Spirit

"The most incomprehensible thing about the universe is that it is comprehensible."
Albert Einstein

Albert Einstein searched for a grand unified theory that would be a "theory of everything." His remarkable and extraordinary conclusions about time and space made him the "village idiot" of Princeton University. At that time, most scientists based their views of time, space, gravity, and matter on Isaac Newton's theory. Einstein must have known the truth of Paradox Twenty ("When people are free to do as they please, they usually imitate each other."), because he thought outside the traditional "box" of science.

The success of Einstein lies in his fundamental beliefs of looking at the simplicity of the world and not being afraid of apparent errors. Einstein saw himself as asking questions only children ask. He did not look for the complexity of issues but the simple coherence of the big picture. His view of life, like that of children, was hopeful and optimistic.

Most of us have lost our childhood wonder and thus, have become unhappy, discontented, and do not live to our potential. We make life too complicated. We forget Robert Fulghum's messages in his book *Everything I need to know I learned in kindergarten.* We forget to "Share everything," "Play fair," and "Don't hit people." We have a tendency to make life too difficult and our minds become too cluttered. Because of this, coaches have to run drills and remind their players to get back to the basics. Teachers go back to teaching the fundamentals in their classrooms. When we forget the simple truths, life seems incomprehensible and we do not grow and evolve.

When we forget the basics and life becomes too overwhelming, we can say to ourselves, "Breathe, breathe." When we forget the fundamentals and become scared, we can say, "One foot in front of the other." If we use these strategies and simplify the moment, we find the flow of life which we had lost.

The basketball great Michael Jordan was in an advertisement campaign where the slogan challenged us to "Be like Mike." Madison Avenue knows we need examples and models to which we can aspire. So let's "Be like Albert," and let simplicity be the engine behind our actions. If you want to comprehend life, get back to the basics. Know the fundamentals. Simplicity is truth. And the truth shall set you free.

When we live this way, we need to be aware of and stay away from overly simplistic, black and white thinking. Rather, we will acknowledge that "simple" truths hold divergent ideas together and help integrate complexity.

All simple truths share a common denominator: get outside of your self and de-power your narcissistic ego. Our ego is not satisfied with the present moment and forever wants more. Its message is, "You are not complete" so we feel like we need more money, more successes, more love, more experiences. This is a lie. The simple truth is we are already complete. If we can relax into our True Self, we will live the paradoxical truths and transcend the pairs of opposites to which most of us identify: good-bad, rich-poor, spiritual-secular. The True Self realizes the kingdom of God is within, we are not separate from God, and we are one with the power in the Universe.

The ultimate truths are really quite simple. Christ said, "Love God and love your neighbor." Buddha said to practice non-attachment. The Native Americans remind us to live connected to nature. Zen Masters tell us to stay present to the moment. If we practice these simple truths, we can start to more fully comprehend life. And, of course, remember from Chapter One that *Simple isn't easy.* Integrating these truths will create a *really* bigger life.

Today, I will let go of one thing that is making my life too busy by _____.
Today, I will spend time in nature by _____.
Today, I will practice loving my neighbor by _____.
Today, I will relax into my True Self by _____.
Today, I will "Be like Albert" by _____.

Today, I will more fully live a simple truth by
_____.

Today, I will _____.

Chapter Seventeen
Mind-Body-Spirit

We need to get beyond ourselves without trying to escape ourselves.

One of the interesting characteristics of young children is that they think the world revolves around them. Many teenagers remain self-absorbed and feel their parents should take care of their every need. Hopefully by adulthood, these egocentric views are abated. Sadly, this is not always true.

To be emotionally healthy, you need to get beyond yourself in two areas. First, get beyond the illusion that "only my needs are important." A good way to measure this is to notice how often you ask the question, "What's in this for me?" If you do, you are probably creating a win-lose situation. Our culture has typically reinforced this outcome. For example, a businessperson can create a larger net income (win) by hurting the environment (lose) or not treating employees fairly (lose).

The healthiest outcome is a win-win solution. This occurs when you create a positive outcome for yourself *and* the other person receives a positive outcome. Ben and Jerry's Ice Cream is a good example. Ben and Jerry made a commitment to be more equitable with salaries. By sharing the financial resources, they created a win for their employees and a win for their company.

Second, get beyond the illusion that you are a separate entity. This is one of ego's strongest and most persistent messages. In reality, you are connected with God, others, and the environment. This realization will help you open your self to God's will and allow you to accept what crosses your path. God wants goodness for everyone. By aligning your self with this truth, you will take care of self *and* take care of others—creating a win-win outcome.

While practicing getting beyond ourselves, we cannot forget about ourselves. We should not jump to the other end of the continuum and look at situations as solely "What can I do for the other person?" Nor should we care for others in a way that damages us, which would prevent us from helping others again in the future. This can lead to unhealthy martyr behaviors. For example, a person who is in a relationship with an alcoholic will give and give and try to help the addict. This could lead to unhealthy behaviors like lying, neglecting oneself, and working to exhaustion. Paradoxically, this "helping" is really enabling the alcoholic and not helping them at all—creating a lose-lose situation.

A good way to get outside oneself is by helping others while maintaining healthy boundaries and taking care of one's self. It takes much wisdom and awareness to find the balance between these two practices, but it can be done.

Tenzin Gyatso, the fourteenth Dalai Lama said, "The foundation of the Buddha's teaching lies in compassion, and the reason for practicing the teachings is to wipe out the persistence of ego, the number-one enemy of compassion." Anne Morrow Lindbergh, writer, pilot, and widow of Charles Lindberg, wrote, "Perhaps middle-age is, or should be, a period of shedding shells: the shell of ambition, the shell of material accumulations and possessions, the shell of ego."

A Hindustani proverb states, "There is nothing noble about being superior to some other person. The true nobility is in being superior to your previous self." When we get beyond ourselves without escaping ourselves, we will more likely create win-win situations, which will create a bigger life for others and our self.

Today, I will ask, "What is good for both of us?" by

_____.

Today, I will maintain healthy personal boundaries while giving myself to others by _____.

Today, I will care for strangers, friends and family, while I still care for myself by _____

_____.

Today, I will be aware of going about my business while also tending to our environment by _____.

Today, I will consciously try to create a win-win solution by _____.

Today, I will bring compassion to my corner of the world by _____.

Today, I will _____.

Chapter Eighteen
Mind-*Body*-Spirit

Bend down to stand tall.

Mother Teresa's life was dedicated to bending down to help people in the streets of India. Even though she was short, Mother Teresa stood tall.

Every day, people bend down to pray for peace, or pray for their enemy. They stand tall.

Others, who brag about their accomplishments or say negative things about people or buy the latest fad, are all *trying* to stand tall. But they fail because it is at the expense of others or by artificial means. Abigail Van Buren wrote in her "Dear Abby" column, "The best index to a person's character is (a) how he treats people who can't do him any good, and (b) how he treats people who can't fight back."

It takes effort to bend down and pick up litter. It takes sweat and labor to bend down to plant a garden or trees for your neighborhood. It takes insight and resolve to overcome ego, which doesn't necessarily like us to help people who can't in return help us. Kind acts create a healthier person, home, community, and nation. They allow individuals and humanity to stand tall. Nineteenth century editor and author Charles Dudley Warner said, "It is one of the beautiful compensations of this life that no one can sincerely try to help another without helping himself."

Buddha said, "Be quick to do good. If you are slow, the mind, delighting in mischief, will catch you." Our egos will make us second guess our innate movement toward kindness. Once we start thinking about helping, our mind will come up with many reasons not to get involved. We can rationalize away anything... even neglecting acts of kindness.

Any act of being humble also creates this paradoxical reaction of standing tall. For example, allowing your spouse, partner, child, or friend to win an argument. Doing the little bit extra at work or home, or doing an act of kindness anonymously means you bend low so they can stand tall. Booker T. Washington, the foremost African-American educator of the nineteenth and twentieth centuries said, "If you want to lift yourself up, lift up someone else."

To be humble is to admit that what sustains us is greater than we are. It is to admit we are not in control. If we are able to keep the faith and do the necessary undertakings through the difficult times, humility reminds us we have not done so alone. To be humble is to do good works, not for personal glory, but for the glory of God.

It is ego that stops us from reaching out to others

and relying more upon God. Our ego has us putting ourselves first and foremost. Ego creates the need to see our selves as separate from others and God. Ego is the root of our pride, self-conceit, and importance. The three letters of ego could stand for **E**dging **G**od **O**ut. Paradoxically, the greater the self-conceit, the less we stand tall. Aesop, the famous Greek writer of fables wrote, "Self-conceit may lead to self-destruction," and "The smaller the mind the greater the conceit."

The difficult question we all have to answer for is "Am I going to follow my narcissistic ego or my spiritual heart?" Ego has us believing we are separate and the center of the universe. Our spiritual heart knows we are all interconnected, and we need to get outside of ourselves and help others.

Author Bernard Bailey said, "When they discover the center of the universe, a lot of people will be disappointed to discover they are not it." Most of us will easily see the humorous truth in this quote. The difficult part is to de-power the ego and truly live tall—by bending down to help others. By doing so we will create a bigger life for ourselves and others.

Today, I will bend down to help Mother Earth by _____.

Today, I will bend down to help a child or a stray animal by _____.

Today, I will ask if I may bend down to anyone who is physically, emotionally, or spiritually not at my eye level by _____.

Today, I will bend down to pray by _____.

Today, I will do a random act of kindness by _____.

Today, I will allow someone else to have the limelight
by _____.
Today, I will _____.

Chapter Nineteen
MInd-*Body*-Spirit

Material goods that we possess tend also to possess us.

Material items are value neutral. They are not good or bad. For example, a plate is just a plate. A car is just a car. A dress is just a dress.

But how many times have our days been ruined when we broke a plate? Or when our car was scratched? Or our garment got stained?

A house is a functional possession. But how many hours of our free time are spent doing yard work, cleaning, re-decorating, painting, and washing? Sometimes a whole weekend is spent tending to the needs of the house.

A computer is a product of our advanced society. It was supposed to make our lives more simple. But how long did you spend trying to figure out how it works? Have you ever been hooked on a new game and it devoured hours of your day? Or have you spent hours trying to de-bug your computer? Our computer and other material possessions serve us—but they also must be served!

Almost everyone has a favorite charity. Have you ever reduced or not made your monthly/yearly donation because you spent your money on material possessions for yourself? Or do you keep working two jobs because you have decided you have to keep living the style in which you are accustomed?

The sad truth is most of us buy things we don't need, with money we don't have, to impress people we don't like or even know.

What does another way of living look like? In the Native American Winnebago culture, when an individual realizes that they do not need certain items any more, they do not have a garage sale and try to make more money. Instead the items are distributed to the community as a way of sharing the wealth. Another example is during the Sun Dance ceremony of the Northern Blackfoot Indians, the richest men of the tribe give away all the possessions which they have accumulated throughout the year to the less advantaged. He who gives away the most is considered the richest man (another paradox). This person demonstrates how hardworking and generous he is, and therefore how wealthy he really is. The desire of the Native American culture is not so much the accumulation of material goods, but the spiritual and relational connections. In contrast, in the Anglo culture, material goods are kept within families, sometimes resulting in family fights over items, amounts, and allocations.

Mother Teresa knew the misery that wealth can create. She said, "In some countries of Asia and Africa, there is mostly material poverty: but in the rich countries of Europe and America there is spiritual poverty and that is more difficult to cure."

A research study compared the happiness levels of lottery winners with adults who had become paraplegic. Their findings are very interesting. At first, the lottery winners were extremely happy and the accident victims depressed. But after about a year, the paraplegics were less depressed and the lottery winners lost their exuberance so both groups were equally content—except the lottery winners reported experiencing less joy in daily events. What is the moral of this research study? The heavy load of the lottery possession made life less satisfying for most of the winners.

An old Chinese expression that says, "Gold dust is precious, but if it gets in the eyes it can cause blindness." This adage can be our motivation to let go of possessing our possessions. They are just possessions. No one is going to remark at your funeral that you drove the latest model automobile.

Live more simply. Share your possessions. You will find yourself living much more freely. And living a bigger life.

Today, I will practice not keeping up with the Jones's.
Today, I will practice living a more simple life.
Today, I will practice not allowing my material goods to possess me.

Today, I will give more freely of my material possessions.

Today, I will spend more time with my children/ spouse/partner/friend, and less time with my possessions.

Today, I will not base a purchase on "wanting."

Today, I will _____.

Chapter Twenty
Mind-*Body*-Spirit

When people are free to do as they please, they usually imitate each other.

We all like to be accepted by others. To varying degrees, we like to blend in and do things to fit in. That is human. We also need to be our own person and develop our own unique abilities.

Many times we lose that balance between acceptance and uniqueness. Usually the balance tips to wanting to be accepted by others and we lose our individuality.

There is a wonderful story of a beloved king, whose castle was on a high hill, overlooking his people. He was so popular that the nearby townspeople sent him gifts daily, and his birthday celebration was enjoyed throughout the kingdom. Everyone loved him for his wisdom and fair judgments.

One day, tragedy struck the town. The water

supply was polluted, and every man, woman and child went insane. Only the king, who had a private spring, was spared.

Soon after the tragedy, the mad townspeople began speaking of how the king was acting "strangely," and how his judgments were poor and his wisdom was a sham. Many even went so far as to say that the king had gone crazy. His popularity soon vanished. No longer did the people bring him gifts or celebrate his birthday.

The lonely king, high on the hill, had no company at all. One day he began to doubt his own judgments and wisdom. He decided to leave the hill and pay a visit to the town. It was a warm day, and he drank from the village fountain.

That night, there was a great celebration. The people all rejoiced, for their beloved king had "regained his sanity."

It takes internal power and personal vision to resist the temptation to follow others. For example, it takes strength for teens to not drink alcohol or do other drugs when they go to a party. An adult has to be strong to say no to a promotion that would take them away from their family during the week. Stephen Covey said, "A leader is the one who climbs the tallest tree, surveys the entire situation, and yells, 'wrong jungle!'" The famous hockey player Wayne Gretzky said, "Most players skate to where the puck is. I skate to where the puck is going to be." This insight and behavior led him to be nicknamed "The Great One," on the ice rink. When we stop going where everyone else is going, and create our own path to something new, we will more likely feel like "The Great One" because we have forsaken our need for conformity and grown into a bigger freedom.

Have you ever noticed that society honors its living conformists and dead troublemakers? Only in hindsight (20-20 vision) will society see the benefit of those who did not imitate others. Jesus, Martin Luther King Jr., and Gandhi are great examples of "troublemakers" who paved the way for the rest of us to live healthier and bigger lives. It will probably feel like a risk to challenge conventional thinking or live outside the box. But to imitate others is to fall into the trap of living a small life. Henry David Thoreau described this state well when he penned: "Most men live lives of quiet desperation."

It is important to honor one self and listen more to one's inner voice than others. It is more important to look within (Paradox Five) than to look to culture for our answers. G.K. Chesterton, one of the greatest thinkers and writers of the twentieth century said, "A dead thing can go with the stream, but only a living thing can go against it." Imitating others usually means deadening our true self (Paradox Twenty). Taking the road less traveled—swimming upstream to what we know is right, will create the life we were created to live—a big life.

Today, I will give less power to society and more power to myself by _____.
Today, I will honor one of my gifts and spend time with it by _____.

Today, I will allow my uniqueness to unfold more fully by _____.

Today, I will hear messages from others and see how they compare or contrast with my values by _____.

Today, I will not drink from the well of insanity by _____.

Today, I will take a calculated risk and follow my own path. Specifically, I will _____.

Today, I will _____.

Chapter Twenty-One
Mind-**Body**-Spirit

Choose a job you love and you will never have to work a day in your life.

The old "round peg in a square hole" theory is so true. If one doesn't match one's gifts and talents with a profession that needs those abilities, work can seem like a four letter word.

If a person is in a job where his or her round peg is trying to fit into a square hole, work is a grind and de-energizing. Sadly, this is true for most people. *The Christian Science Monitor* interviewed business futurist Joyce Gioia, who stated, "Approximately 72 percent of people who are employed in the United States today don't like their jobs."

The president of a local college gave a talk where he said the Latin derivative of the word vocation is vocatioi, which means "a calling." He said he believed the goal of higher education should be to make each student a better listener so he or she could hear their calling.

Having a different attitude in your current job is a way to live this paradoxical truth. A wonderful spiritual practice is to appreciate each task, and give the glory to God. You may not like the job, but you can choose to overlay it with the task of bringing your authentic self to it more fully. This is like the story about the man who is cutting stone for a project that involves hard physical labor. Other workers say they are cutting and moving stone. The man with a different attitude says, "I am building a cathedral."

To many people, work is arduous and an exhausting experience. They think the answer to their exhaustion is rest. The deeper answer is to not do the things that exhaust you, but do the things you love. Work can be an energizing and rewarding experience. There is a popular adage, "Figure out what you want to do; then get someone to pay you for it."

The movie *Office Space* depicts the cynicism of people who don't enjoy their jobs. The story centers on a man in his thirties who despises his work. He says to a co-worker, "Each day of work is progressively worse than the day before, so every time you see me, that's the worst day of my life."

Sadly, this struggle to handle the monotony, and find meaning and fulfillment resonates with most people. Many people stay stuck in unrewarding work because they are making good salaries, or they are waiting until they're fully vested in a retirement program, or they fear making a change. They become manacled by velvet handcuffs: they are made ineffective and powerless because of the economic trappings that surround them.

Glenn Frey sings in the Eagle's song, *Already Gone*, "So often times it happens that we live our lives in chains, And we never even know we have the key." Freedom is in our own hands. If we take a risk and share our vision with someone else, maybe she will have an insight or know of a more fitting job. If we take a risk and talk to someone in the field we want to work, maybe he will build a bridge and help make the transition. If one makes room in one's life for the things one loves, this opening will more fully allow the better job to appear.

Take the time to know what your true gifts are, then trust the Universe that someone will pay you for that work. Then do the necessary sharing, working, connecting, and praying to help make that job become a reality.

Authenticity is aligning your passions and purpose with your work. Authentic work doesn't feel like work. It can be a flow of our natural talents, empowering to others and ourselves. Mythologist and author Joseph Campbell said, "If you follow your bliss, you put yourself on a kind of track that has been there all the while, waiting for you, and the life that you ought to be living is the one you are living." Author Kahil Gibran wrote something very similar: "When you are born, your work is placed in your heart. There is music in you. Don't die with your music in you." Life is too big for it not to happen.

Today, I will accept the fact that I don't have to stay my job by _____.

Today, I will mentally create the ideal job for myself by _____.

Today, I will pray for that specific job by _____.

Today, I will start creating that job by _____.

Today, I will start the process of aligning my "square peg" in a "square hole" by _____.

Today, I will quiet my mind so I may hear my calling by _____.

Today, I will _____.

Chapter Twenty-Two
Mind-**Body**-Spirit

Non-verbal communication speaks loudly.

Shrugged shoulders. Arms that are crossed against the chest. Eyes that show indifference. Tapping fingers.

When you experience one of these non-verbal forms of communication, how does it make you feel?

Open arms. A twinkle in an eye. An outstretched hand. Squared shoulders.

When you experience one of these non-verbal forms of communication, how does it make you feel?

Research shows that the words constitute only 7% of any message that is sent. Non-verbal communication is close to 50% of the message! (The remainder being environment and vocal intonations.) Ralph Waldo Emerson wrote in his essay on Self Reliance: "Men imagine they communicate their virtue only by overt actions and words. They do not see that virtue, or its opposite, emits a breath every moment."

Non-verbal communication speaks loudly.   It is very important to be aware of what your body is "saying." If you are aware of why you have a frown on your face, you can work through your unhappiness or anger before you pass it on to someone else. Clenched hands are an important indicator that anger is rising. These non-verbal cues will help you own your feelings, and then deal with them…before you deal them to someone else.

Each one of us represents a sermon. We may not be preaching from a pulpit, but every movement, voice intonation, period of silence, and gesture is a form of communication in which our "congregation" is aware. Is our "sermon" to our family members loving and compassionate? Is our "sermon" to work associates meaningful and inspirational? Is our "sermon" to strangers positive and kindhearted?   St. Francis of Assisi said, "Preach constantly. If necessary, use words."

Understanding and applying non-verbal communication is extremely helpful to your personal growth, career, and relationships.   Often when a person is thought to have great intuition about other people, his or her understanding is actually due to watchful and thorough observation of other people's non-verbal communication. Ralph Waldo Emerson's famous quote, "What you do speaks so loud that I cannot hear what you say," speaks to this fact. A person attuned to knowing and reading another's non-verbal communication will pick up important points that others miss.   In fact, the non-verbal communication is so "loud" that the words don't mean much.

Did you know the body cannot lie? Our minds and words can easily create lies. But non-verbal communication through our body always tells the truth. For example, a child who wants to get out of trouble might tell a lie. But when he does, he always bites his lip. An astute parent will "listen" more to the child's lip biting and less to his words. Or a co-worker who tries to make a troublesome situation sound good, but her foot is wagging the entire time she talks. Her words mean less than the anxious foot that shakes back and forth.

English novelist of the Victorian era, Charles Dickens penned, "Electric communication will never be a substitute for the face of someone who with their soul encourages another person to be brave and true." Practice sending positive non-verbal messages. Practice matching your non-verbal message with your verbal message. Practice giving excellent "sermons." You will feel better...and the receiver of your messages will feel better, too. Everyone's world will become a little bit bigger.

Today, I will send positive non-verbal messages.
Today, I will practice matching my non-verbal communication with my verbal communication.
Today, I will be more fully aware of the adage, "actions speak louder than words".
Today, I will put a little more bounce in my walk.
Today, I will smile to the people that cross my path.
Today, I will share an inspirational and loving "sermon."
Today, I will _____.

Chapter Twenty-Three
Mind-*Body*-Spirit

The act of freeing oneself can bind one to that new reality.

Rabbi Zalman Schachter-Shalomi, founder of the P'nai Or Religious Fellowship said, "Every tradition begins in the white heat of transcendent realization, then gradually over time suffers hardening of the religious arteries through the unavoidable process of institutionalization." Protestants chose an act of freedom when they left the Catholic Church. Now, one's spiritual journey can evolve to being bound by a Protestant church's committees, tenets, or unspoken norms of conformity.

We have a tendency to identify with our limitations. For example, you think your body can take only fifteen minutes of exercise. Or, you think you can only donate two percent of your income to charities. A person may think he has to work more than others. This type of thinking creates detrimental cages in your life. In other words, you will find your self in a "cage" that is making your life small. The door to the cage is always open. But most choose to stay in their cage. Some take a great risk and leave their cage. This is an incredible act of courage and results in freedom. The paradox is, in time, because of attachments to outcomes, they will inevitably move to a bigger cage—but still a cage.

A man can make a grand act of freedom and leave his job in which he feels stuck. That person can go back to school, or create a new job in which his gifts are more honored. But that new reality, that was once freedom, can then be another cage from which he needs to escape. For example, a businessman leaves his workplace for another that he thinks is better suited to him. Once there, he finds tension in the new office over the direction of a certain project. He is determined to sign up a certain number of clients. Over time, he has lost his freedom and has created a new cage.

A mom feels overwhelmed working outside the home and raising her children. She wants the freedom to stay home with her children. This mom resigns from her workplace, only to feel overwhelmed again and feels the four walls of her home are a prison. The mountains of dirty clothes, piles of dirty dishes, never-ending meals to prepare, chauffeur service, and maid duties are done with no appreciation and reward.

Cages are created because of our propensity to attach to outcomes. The mom could get attached to many things: how her children should act, how long a child should nap, or what the children should eat. When the children do not live up to mom's attachments/outcomes, she loses her freedom. Going with the flow and practicing non-attachment will open the cage door and create freedom.

Buddha said "Life is suffering." He stated the cause of suffering is from psychological and emotional attachments. We tend to never be satisfied and to crave, thirst, and desire for things to be other than what they are. There are two "flavors" of not being happy with the way things are: desire and aversion. Desire is the attachment of wanting more, being greedy, and possessive love. Aversion includes hatred, resentment, and anger. The release from attachment is by letting go, of being non-attached to outcomes and to the self-defeating liking and disliking of what crosses our paths. If you want to do something better, do it better. But do not be attached to any new result.

The point is *not* that it is useless to leave our cage. The point is to be aware of our attachments...because they will automatically put us back in the cage and we will lose our freedom. And, as Alexander Graham Bell said: "We sometimes look so longingly at the closed door that we miss the one that's opening." Find the open door, enter in a non-attached manner, and live a bigger life.

Today, I will name a cage in which I am bound by
_____.

Today, I will find the door and know I can leave the cage by _____.

Today, I will name the attachment that is keeping me inside a cage by _____.

Today, I will let go of that attachment and move toward freedom by _____.

Today, I will move toward freedom in an area in which I feel trapped by _____.

Today, I will create the theme of "freedom" in my life by _____.

Today, I will _____.

Chapter Twenty-Four
Mind-*Body*-Spirit

If you aim at nothing you are bound to hit it.

The archer aims at the bull's eye. The golfer aims for the hole. The racecar driver accelerates toward the checkered flag.

Every person, at every minute of the day, is aiming or working toward something. It could be healthy or unhealthy, conscious or unconscious, growth or stagnation—the movement is in one direction or the other.

Many people are goal oriented; they make New Year's Resolutions, write out to do lists, or use planners. Many others live a conditional existence of compulsions and habits. These daily behaviors are repeated so many times that they create ruts. These people quit aiming for anything new, so they stay underemployed, unhappy, and stuck. They are like a deer who stares at a car's headlights: frozen, not knowing which way to move. So they do nothing, which creates a miserable, unhappy, small life.

John C. Maxwell, in his book *The 21 Irrefutable Laws of Leadership*, states that the first law is the Law of the Lid. "Leadership ability is the lid that determines a person's level of effectiveness. The lower an individual's ability to lead, the lower the lid of potential. The higher the leadership, the greater the effectiveness. You can find smart, talented, successful people who are able to go only so far because of the limitations of their leadership." This paradox is true in leading others and it is also true in leading yourself.

To be able to create a personal vision and lead yourself out of a deep rut, you must look inward (Paradox Five) and start the process of knowing yourself and your value system. No longer can direction be found by looking at others. You must find your own internal compass by re-claiming your gifts and talents and find a job that will pay you for using them (Paradox Twenty-one). If you are unable to create a vision, listen to your inner voice, take a risk and shoot for a goal. Aim high.

Henry David Thoreau said, "In the long run, you hit only what you aim for." If you are aiming at the same old thing, it is as if you are aiming at nothing. And then you're bound to hit it.

Yogi Berra said, "When you come to a fork in the road, take it." This humorous line makes us laugh. Lewis Carroll in *Alice in Wonderland* wrote, "When Alice approached a fork in the road, she saw a Cheshire cat. She asked, 'What road should I take?' Replied the

Cheshire cat, 'Where do you want to go?' Alice said, 'It doesn't matter.' Then the Cheshire cat said, 'If it doesn't matter where you want to go, then it doesn't matter what road you take.'" Carroll's quote should make us stop and wonder if we really know what road we're on. Is the road taking us the direction that we learned from our parents? Is it a direction that culture states is important? Is it a direction that was right for us many years ago, but one that we have outgrown?

Seeing results from our actions help us continue to take aim at our goals. But sometimes immediate feedback is not available. Mahatma Gandhi said, "You may never know what results come of your action, but if you do nothing there will be no result."

Author and motivational speaker, Zig Zigler said, "Lack of direction, not lack of time, is the problem. We all have twenty-four hour days." If we really want to live a big life, we need to honor our self, take a risk, and take aim for a new direction in our life.

Today, I will aim a little bit higher by _____.

Today, I will make a short-term goal by _____.

Today, I will start climbing out of my rut by _____.

Today, I will raise the lid of my personal leadership by _____.

Today, I will be conscious of where I am going in my life by _____.

Today, I will take a risk by _____.

Today, I will _____.

Chapter Twenty-Five
Mind-*Body*-Spirit

Close your eyes so you can see.

Many of us live too much by our five senses. We believe something only if we can see it. We think something exists only if we can touch it, smell it, taste it, or hear it.

Our lives can be so much more than a five-sensory experience—if we let intuition, our inner guide, do its job. This sense-of-knowing the right thing to do can help us find our path. Intuition can help us come up with creative solutions. But this can only happen if we get out of our minds and live more in our hearts.

In the movie *Aladdin*, princess Jasmine is having a hard time deciding if she should be with Aladdin. Her five senses tell her that he is a young street urchin, which does not fit her current worldview. Aladdin finally asks Jasmine the very pointed question, "Tell me princess, now when did you last let your heart decide?" Aladdin knows true vision comes from the heart.

It is very typical to become stumped and not know how to resolve a problem. Like a car stuck in mud, the harder you accelerate, the deeper the rut you create. When you are experiencing this, while you're trying to find new practical solutions, it is helpful to trust God and ask for an answer. God's answer to your prayer can take many different forms. For example, have you ever had the experience of being at a library or bookstore and having a book "jump out" at you? Or have you run into a friend who you hadn't seen in a while? This "chance" encounter helped you with a problem you were experiencing. Psychologist Carl Jung wrote about these serendipitous events. He believed there were no coincidences in life. He said that there are synchronistic events that occur at the specific time we need guidance. Christians believe the Holy Spirit is always working in our lives in the same manner. Second Corinthians states, "We walk by faith, not by sight."

Trust walks are a good group building exercise. In this adventure, one person is blindfolded while another person takes him or her for a walk. The guide communicates in detail the immediate environment so as to make the walk safe for the other person. The main purpose is to help group members rely on each other, which will build trust. Afterwards while processing the experience, most of the blindfolded people shared that their trust of the other person increased. But they had also heard sounds from nature, felt subtle changes in temperature, and smelled different things.

The fully visual people missed all these experiences. By bringing other senses into play, the blindfolded people's walk was more full of life.

Many inventors have stated that when they were stuck on a project, the solution to the problem came when they quit using their rational mind. Progress was finally made when they relied more on their intuition. Bill Gates said, "Often you have to rely on intuition." Jonas Salk, developer of polio vaccine, said, "Intuition will tell my thinking mind where to look next." And, Albert Einstein said, "The only real valuable thing is intuition."

There is more information to access than what the rational mind picks up through our five senses. Three-time Academy Award winner Ingrid Bergman said, "You must trust your intuition—you must trust the small voice inside you which tells you exactly what to say, what to decide." Psychologist Dr. Joyce Brothers said, "Trust your hunches. They're usually based on facts filed away just below the conscious level."

The question Aladdin asked Jasmine is a wonderful question to ponder. This can help us find balance in our decision-making process. Close your eyes. Look within. Listen. Trust. With time, you will see life more clearly. You will live a bigger life.

Today, I will make a decision with my heart by _____.

Today, I will close my eyes and listen to the sounds around me by _____.

Today, I will honor the synchronistic events that cross my path by _____.

Today, I will journal about a tug or pull I have felt in my life _____.

Today, I will process with a friend or a professional a dream I have by _____.

Today, I will try to make decisions in a more balanced way with my head and heart by _____.

Today, I will _____.

Chapter Twenty-Six
Mind-*Body*-Spirit

Those who exclude others end up excluding themselves.

We humans tend to judge that which we don't understand. By judging others, we usually condemn them and push them outside our circle of acceptance.

Fear of the unknown causes us to react in this exclusionary way. Unhealthy thoughts can fill our mind because a person follows a different religion, has a different skin color, or a different sexual orientation. Other differences include socio-economic status, type of dress, or communication style.

These practices of exclusion deny us many new growth opportunities. We need to take off our blinders and open up our field of vision. We need to be fortified, not terrified. New ways of seeing the world will only strengthen and enrich us.

When is the last time you reached out and tried

to create a new friendship? Stagnation will occur by staying in our current circle of acceptance. Personal growth will occur if we include others—different from ourselves—in our lives.

One dynamic that physics teaches is that things are either growing and evolving, or contracting and getting smaller. This truth also applies to our lives. If we are excluding others, not growing and learning, our world will become smaller and constrictive. In fact, we will start to care only about maintaining the status quo. That is like rearranging the furniture on the Titanic…it might look better, but it's heading for a disastrous outcome.

Author and psychotherapist Wayne Dyer wrote, "When you judge another, you do not define them, you define yourself." This definition of your self will include being narrow-minded and critical—which will keep people away and create a small world for your self.

In the dedication of his book, *In One Era and Out the Other,* author Sam Levenson wrote to his new grandchild, "We leave you a tradition with a future. The tender loving care of human beings will never become obsolete. People, even more than things, have to be restored, renewed, revived, reclaimed and redeemed and redeemed and redeemed. Never throw out anybody….As you grow older you will discover that you have two hands. One for helping yourself, and the other for helping others."

We are involved in different groups during the course of our days. Our family, friends, work cohorts, church committees, civic clubs, and book clubs, are examples of these groups. Sociologists say that all groups go through the same stages of group development. One way to describe the stages is; forming, storming, norming, and performing. After the hard work of resolving conflicts, taking risks, and learning to trust the other group members, authenticity and acceptance of differences occurs in the "performing" stage. The group starts giving less attention to status and more attention to the ideas and unique abilities of *all* members. Each member can now be known and treated as an individual, and the unique abilities of each member can be used for the betterment of the group. This highest level of group development cannot be reached if members are excluded and not allowed to share their distinct strengths and talents. The synergy of working together and creating something big will only occur by including all members.

Today, I will open my circle of acceptance by _____.
Today, I will purposefully seek out someone who is
    different from me by _____.
Today, I will love my neighbor as myself by _____.
Today, I will include someone in a conversation, or a
    lunch, that I normally would not by _____.
Today, I will quit worrying about maintaining the
    status quo, and learn a new way of interacting in
    the world by _____.
Today, I will create a growth experience by _____.
Today, I will _____.

Chapter Twenty-Seven
Mind-**Body**-Spirit

A man grows most tired by standing still.
Chinese Proverb

Many adults who have responsibilities of work and family, lose the habit of exercising. Even on weekends when they don't have as much to do, they tend to sit. This more sedentary lifestyle is tiring. They yawn, cat nap, and lay around with no energy. If they pull them self off the couch and go for a run or play tennis, they arrive back home with lots of new energy.

This phenomenon is also true with adolescents. Many teens state that they are bored and have nothing to do. They watch television, play video games, or lie around which makes them tired and depressed. The teens that get a part-time job, or find a hobby, or play a sport, are happier and more full of life. Research shows that teens that are involved in extracurricular activities or work up to fifteen hours a week, perform better in school. One of the main reasons is because they are in the habit of accomplishing something.

Being sedentary is linked to a wide range of debilitating ailments like diabetes, arthritis pain, digestive problems, osteoporosis, and physical frailty. Being inactive is associated with potential killers like high blood pressure, high cholesterol, strokes, and heart attacks. Research shows that even being moderately active can reduce the risk of coronary artery disease and other chronic diseases.

There's nothing more tiring than doing nothing. Our minds also grow tired and lazy if they aren't pushed and exercised. If television is the most thought-provoking and strenuous brain activity for the day, becoming a couch potato could be a reality. Exercising one's mind could be learning how to meditate or playing a board game. Crossword puzzles or reading a new book are stimulating and lead to growth experiences.

One of the many wonderful characteristics of Mother Teresa was decisiveness. She was an advocate of not waiting to do good, but to take immediate action. She would often tell the Sisters: "Charity begins today. Today somebody is suffering, today somebody is in the street, today somebody is hungry. Our work is for today, yesterday has gone, tomorrow has not yet come. We see a need, we go to meet it; at least, we do something about it."

Helping others and getting things accomplished is energizing. Exercise is invigorating. Work can be exciting. Helping another will help your self (Paradox Thirty-five). Step out and exert energy—physically or mentally, and you'll be less tired. You don't have to run the Boston Marathon tomorrow. Start with incremental steps.

Volunteering at a non-profit agency, starting a new hobby, and taking the dog for a walk are all stimulating. You don't have to save the world, but you can help one other person—even your self. As the Chinese proverb says, "Don't be afraid of going slow but be afraid of not going at all."

Lord Chesterfield, English author and statesman said, "It is an undoubted truth, that the less one has to do, the less time one finds to do it in." Chesterfield writes paradoxically about the need to create forward motion in your life. If you fall into a rut of sitting in your easy chair at home, you won't find the time or have the energy to parent your children in a healthy manner, finish a project, or meet new people. If you choose to be active, you will start the process of having a happier and bigger life.

Today, I will exercise at least ten minutes (A ten minute walk counts!).
Today, I will find a new hobby.
Today, I will take a walk around my neighborhood.
Today, I will read a book.
Today, I will learn a new word.
Today, I will clean a room with the mindset that it will give me more energy.
Today, I will _____.

Chapter Twenty-Eight
Mind-**Body**-Spirit

Tomorrow is built today.

Reincarnation is a basic belief of Buddhism and Hinduism. In this perspective, people's past life experiences affect their present day life and future lives. The deeds done today will affect their lives in the future. There is a wonderful story of a Buddhist novice who studied under a great teacher who could "see" past and future lives. Often the student would ask the teacher to share what his future reincarnations will look like. The teacher would always smile and answer, "If you want to know what your future life will be, look at your present thoughts and actions."

This truth from another culture and another century remains true today. Our work today will affect our tomorrow. Philosopher, historian and author Will Durant said, "The future never just happened. It was created."

Many children's fairy tales share the reality of this paradox. The story of the Three Little Pigs is a great example. Each pig built a house that took varying degrees of time and effort. The first pig took the easiest and fastest route and built his house with straw. The second pig also took the quick and easy path and built his with sticks. The third little pig was wise and not afraid of hard work. He built his house with bricks. As we know, the wolf blew down the houses made quickly with straw and sticks (without any thought of tomorrow), and ate those pigs for dinner. The wolf was unsuccessful blowing down the house constructed with bricks. The pig that planned for his future lived a long and happy life.

High school State Championships, college bowl games, and Super Bowls are won by the athletes training in the weight rooms, running up and down steps, and practicing the plays. Every day the athletes are conditioning their minds and bodies to be successful in the big game. Their daily practices and workouts build better performances for tomorrow.

This paradox is just as real with the dynamic of money. Over 50% of Americans will not have saved any money for retirement by the time they turn sixty-five. In other words, they will be broke. Napoleon Hill states in *Law of Success*, "The saving of money is solely a habit." He goes on to say, "It is literally true that man, through the Law of Habit, shapes his own personality. Through repetition, any act indulged in a few times becomes a habit and the mind appears to be nothing more than a mass of motivating forces growing out of our daily habits."

If one decides to create a *daily* habit of saving a portion of her income, the *tomorrow* of her retirement years will be a time of financial abundance rather than a time of financial hardship.

Buddha said, "What we are today comes from our thoughts of yesterday, and our present thoughts build our life of tomorrow. Our life is the creation of our mind." One of Steven Covey's seven habits of successful living is "start with the end in mind." If you know how you want something to turn out, start with that mental image and then work towards that final product. In other words, if you mentally know how you want your "tomorrow," start working on that "today."

Dallas Cowboys former football coach Tom Landry, said, "Today, you have 100% of your life left." What you do today is important because you are exchanging a day of your life for it—and you're building your tomorrow. Make sure you are building a big life.

Today, I will be aware of my thoughts and actions (because I know they create my future), by ____.

Today, I will picture my "tomorrow" and work on creating that "today" by _____.

Today, I will start saving for my retirement by

_____.

Today, my efforts will be more like the little pig who built his house with bricks by _____

_____.

Today, I will be more mindful of what I sow, because I know that is what I will reap, by _____.

Today, I will be the captain of my ship and sail to the port of my choice by _____ _____.

Today, I will _____.

Chapter Twenty-Nine
Mind-*Body*-Spirit

You don't know what you have until it's gone.

How many times have you wanted to visit or call someone, but didn't follow through because you got busy with something else? How many times have you said no to your children's playful requests because "there will be time for that later."

Our children grow up quickly and soon won't want to play with us. Our society is very mobile. Friends can move or be transferred before we re-connect with them. We can miss out on the important parts of life when we forget the impermanent nature of our existence.

Harry Chapin wrote poignantly about this in the song *Cat's in the Cradle.* The father starts the story by stating "My child arrived just the other day,...But there were planes to catch, and bills to pay. He learned to walk while I was away." Later, the little boy asks, "When you coming home, dad?" His dad responds, "I don't know when. But we'll have a good time then."

Dad's behaviors continued until his son went away to college. Then he realized this paradoxical truth and he tried to interact with his son. Sadly, the son was caught in the same lie and they never re-connected.

Joni Mitchell's 1970 *Big Yellow Taxi* gives many funny and biting examples of this paradox. The first example is "They paved paradise and they put up a parking lot. With a pink hotel, a boutique and a swinging hot spot." She goes on to say, "They took all the trees and put them in a tree museum." She asks the farmers to "Put away that D.D.T. now, give me spots on my apples, but leave me the birds and the bees." Lastly, she writes, "Late last night, I heard the screen door slam. And a big yellow taxi took away my old man." Mitchell ties these all together with the chorus, "Don't it always seem to go, that you don't know what you've got till it's gone."

"Sometimes I'm so busy seeing what I don't have, that I don't see what I do have," is an Al-Anon saying. The practice to overcome this negative thinking is to focus on what you do have. Focus on the good traits of family members. Focus on the money you have and how you can use it most wisely. Focus on the positive interactions you've had with friends. Focus on the legs you have for walking. Nineteenth century cleric and writer Charles Caleb Colton said, "True friendship is like sound health; the value of it is seldom known until it is lost."

Wise people have shared strategies to awaken

us so we don't miss our children growing up, or the potential of each day. German philosopher Fredrich Nietzsche wrote, "We should consider every day lost on which we have not danced at least once." English novelist and poet G.K. Chesterton wrote, "The way to love anything is to realize that it might be lost."

Take time to enjoy the beauty and fragrance of the flowers before they die. Take a walk in the park before winter settles in. If you see an injustice, write or call your local, state, or national political representative. Be thankful and more aware of your eyesight, and your ability to walk. Call a friend for coffee or lunch. Call a grandparent, parent, relative, or friend today— there might not be a tomorrow.

Life is precious. Life is fleeting. Live life. Take a risk. Start to live a bigger life.

Today, I will take the time to embrace what crosses my path by _____.

Today, I will honor the positive thoughts that cross my mind by _____.

Today, I will re-connect with a friend by _____.

Today, I will let someone know I love him or her by _____.

Today, I will make a gratitude list by _____.

Today, I will seize the day by _____.

Today, I will _____.

Chapter Thirty
Mind-**Body**-Spirit

Your greatest strength is also your greatest weakness.

One of the greatest strengths of living paradoxical truths is that one embraces "both-and" thinking and lets go of "either-or" thinking. The image that can help us fully learn and integrate this truth is the Yin-Yang symbol (defined in Chapter Eleven). To be a whole person, we need to find balance and embrace the whole continuum of life.

Many people live one-sided lives. For example, the strength of being competitive, strong, and achievement-oriented served a businessman well during work hours. He built a big, successful company that hired many people in the community. And yet, when he played racquetball, this competitive strength became brutal and obnoxious to the point that no one enjoyed playing with him.

The strength of being selfless, other-oriented, and taking care of others served a mother and her children well. The children were well nurtured and loving. And yet, when she served on a church committee, she did more work than anyone else and started to feel like a martyr.

A person with extroverted preferences tends to get his energy from the outer world of people and things. An extrovert processes his thoughts externally by talking. An extrovert will be very verbal during a meeting because that is his preferred method to process information. This is a great strength because his ideas will be known. This strength is a double-edged sword and can get him into trouble because he doesn't screen his sharing and tends to say too much. The extrovert might leave a meeting and say, "I wish I had not shared..."

In these three examples, the businessman's lesson is to lighten up, have fun, and build relationships. The mother's lesson is to establish healthy boundaries and say "no." The extrovert needs to process the subject internally before he talks. If we stay stuck in an area and overly develop a certain style of living, these strengths will become our weaknesses.

Sometimes when we get stuck in life and our problem solving strategies are not working, we will utilize those tactics to an even stronger degree. We are usually baffled when the results of these efforts create even more of a problem. Marge Piercy, an American poet, novelist, and social activist said, "My strengths and weaknesses are twins in the same womb." Stepping outside our habits and learning new behaviors will help birth healthier ways of solving problems and living.

The great psychologist Carl Jung thought neurosis resulted from a one-sided personality development. For example, not being able to balance assertiveness and nurturing will create either a bully or a martyr. Not being able to balance a structured lifestyle with a flexible one will create either rigidity or irresponsibility.

Jung also said the first half of one's life is to fully develop one's innate personality. The second half of one's life is to work on the other side—the least preferred personality traits. To integrate this truth means we have to acknowledge and embrace the personality qualities we more naturally exhibit. Then we need to name and practice the opposite personality characteristics that we don't live as often. When we practice the least preferred traits, they will serve to complement our more intrinsic traits. In so doing, our strengths will less likely become our weaknesses. We will live well-rounded and bigger lives.

Today, I will bring more fully into the light the personality traits that tend to govern my life. I will _____.

Today, I will name a healthy personality trait I see in someone else that I think will help me live a more balanced lifestyle by _____.

Today, I will quit blaming someone else for my unhappiness and find the characteristic in me that will help me lead a happier life. I will _____.

Today, I will consciously practice the opposite of my strongest personality trait by _____.

Today, I will ask my spouse/partner/friend which personality trait would help me lead a more balanced life. Specifically, I will _____.

Today, I will more fully learn how to live a trait from the "other side" of my personality. Specifically, I will _____.

Today, I will _____.

Chapter Thirty-One
Mind-**Body**-Spirit

The biggest struggle is to stop struggling.

Work is a necessary ingredient of life. Being responsible, putting in sweat equity, and struggling for what we believe in is important. There is merit in being captain of your own ship. *And* there is another component of life that is also important and we usually forget about: faith in God. The apostle Paul wrote that both faith and works are important. Paul's point is both-and thinking: faith and works.

Embracing both-and thinking and finding balance is a daily practice. For example, most of us live with the illusion that we are in control. If something is wrong we believe we must struggle to fix it. We might work hard to hang on to a relationship that is no longer healthy. But the faith component may say if we let go of the relationship and pray for guidance and wisdom for the situation, we might find the psychological space that would allow a new person to enter our life.

Acts of faith will necessarily include letting go and surrendering to God's will. Oprah Winfrey stated in her 2000 commencement address to the graduates of Salem College: "What I know for sure is, you cannot run your life without surrender...Surrender to the universe's dream for you..."

Surrendering is not an act of defeat—it is an act of power. It is an act of letting go of what is not good for us. It is a forward movement into who we truly are and aligning our purpose with God's purpose for us.

Many people are sad or depressed because they have heavy burdens. They have been struggling for years, trying to fix or escape their problems. They have been unsuccessful and now feel worse than ever. Many different healing and coping strategies are available to help them. The one that usually seems the most foreign is to stop struggling so much and hand their problems over to God.

There is more going on in our lives than meets the eye. There is a Higher Being who is benevolent and always wants what is best for us. If we can trust, and admit that the problem is bigger than we are, we can stop struggling so much and give it up to a higher spiritual source.

There are many strategies that can help us stop the overwhelming struggle. For example, write your thoughts and feelings in a letter—one that you will not send. Be brutally honest in the letter and then share it with a trusted person or ritually burn it, symbolically letting go of the struggle. Another strategy is to take the burden out of your "in box" and put it into the hands of your Higher Being. If you take the burden back, gently give it again to your God. Or, write the struggle on a balloon, and release it to the wind, watching it fly further and further away from you. Even create a funeral, where you will symbolically bury the burden—putting it to rest for eternity.

The Buddha stated that the cause of all suffering is attachment. If we are struggling with a problem, we are attached to it by the fact we are trying to push it away, or manipulate it to a certain outcome. The release of suffering comes from letting go—not with an "I don't care" attitude, but one that is compassionate for yourself and others.

Letting go, or surrendering, is a practice of finding the balance between faith and works. It is a practice that includes being mindful of being responsible and doing the necessary work, and being aware of allowing God and the goodness of the Spirit to guide and help you. If you feel you are working too hard and life is a struggle, this is a possible sign that you have taken control and are not allowing the goodness of God to assist you. If you find yourself too cavalier and relying on others or God too much, edge yourself closer to the middle way and start taking action. This practice will start an accumulation of wisdom that will guide you to a closer balance between faith and works. You will live a bigger life with fewer struggles.

Today, I will admit that I am stuck in my struggles. I will _____.

Today, I will practice letting go of the struggles by
_____.

Today, I will more fully trust in my Higher Power by
_____.

Today, I will consciously give a problem over to God
by _____.

Today, I will acknowledge my unease with a situation,
and then stop trying to "fix" it. Specifically, I will
_____.

Today, I will practice surrendering by _____.
Today, I will _____.

Chapter Thirty-Two

Mind-***Body***-Spirit

The price tag of success is failure.

Success and failure can be easily seen in sports activities. For example, failure can be spotted when we hit the tennis ball into the net or slice the golf ball into the rough. Gathering the information within the failure can help us move closer to success. Correcting the failures will create better performances.

Babe Ruth hit 714 home runs—a record that was untouchable for many years. The great Ruth also had more failures than any other baseball player. He struck out 1330 times. If he were not swinging for the fences, he would not have reached such milestones during his career.

As Francis T. Vincent, Jr., the eighth commissioner of Major League Baseball observed, such failure is necessary: "Baseball teaches us, or has taught most of us, how to deal with failure. We learn at a very young age that failure is the norm in baseball and, precisely because we have failed, we hold in high regard those who fail less often—those who hit safely in one out of three chances and become star players. I also find it fascinating that baseball, alone in sport, considers errors to be part of the game, part of its rigorous truth."

In our daily life, we will fall short of a desired behavior. We may overreact in our parenting or do poorly during a sales presentation. Within these failings is the information for more successful behaviors next time.

Samuel Smiles, a nineteenth century Scottish political reformist and author of *Self-Help*, wrote "We learn wisdom from failure much more than success. We often discover what will do by finding out what will not do: and probably he who never made a mistake never made a discovery."

Thomas Edison was one of the world's most successful inventors. He was awarded 1,368 separate and distinct patents during his lifetime. Along with those incredible successes were even more failures. Edison once said, "If I find 10,000 ways something won't work, I haven't failed. I am not discouraged because every wrong attempt discarded is just one more step forward." He realized this paradoxical truth in his own life, learned from his mistakes, and created an incredible number of successes. Edison went on to say, "Unfortunately, many of life's failures are experienced by people who did not realize how close they were to success when they gave up."

Once we realize how much information is in each of our failures, we will more likely embrace the shortcomings and move closer to successes. Wendell Phillips, an 1833 graduate of Harvard Law School who dedicated his life to anti-slavery causes, said "What is defeat? Nothing but education; nothing but the first step to something better."

Our ego does not like failure. Our ego likes to shine in successes. It takes strength to de-power the ego and admit we fell short and step up to the plate again. Author James Rollins wrote, "Wringing your hands only stops you from rolling up your sleeves." It's easier to place blame on someone else and not try again. If we understand that there is much information to discern within our mistakes, it's easier to risk and take another stab at success.

We need a disciplined mind to practice accepting failure and taking another risk. The Buddha said, "An untrained mind is your greatest enemy, while a disciplined mind is your greatest friend." Accepting our failures, not buying into our feelings of embarrassment or inadequacy, takes perseverance and self-control.

Thomas Watson, who built IBM into a computer giant, said "If you want to succeed, double your failure rate." This will get you closer to living a big life.

Today, I will embrace a failure that occurs in my life by _____.

Today, I will look closer at the failure and learn its lesson by _____.

Today, I will practice a new way of being based on the advice found in the failures by _____.

Today, I will be okay if I "strike out" while I'm "swinging for the fences." Specifically, I will _____.

Today, I will realize I am a step closer to success each time a failure occurs by _____.

Today, I will be gentle on myself while I incrementally move closer to more functional behaviors. Specifically, I will _____.

Today, I will _____.

Chapter Thirty-Three
Mind-*Body*-Spirit

"Little strokes fell great oaks."
Benjamin Franklin

Most of us have perceived big obstacles in our lives: credit card debt, children misbehaving, personal unhappiness, a dead-end job, or unrewarding relationships. Sometimes the issues feel so big, that we deny our personal power and stop our efforts of resolution. This creates stagnation and angst in our lives.

Usually, the biggest monthly expense is rent and the biggest debt most people will incur is their home mortgage. This monthly payment is usually budgeted, and because we need a roof over our heads, it is paid first without exception. Interestingly, we don't perceive our biggest debt as an insurmountable obstacle because we handle it with structure, discipline, and responsibility.

Most of the obstacles listed in the first paragraph

are not bigger in scope than our mortgage. The word "perceived" was used in the first paragraph because we do not handle them in the same healthy manner as we do the mortgage or rent, so we mistake them as bigger than what they really are.

An article in *Science of Mind* shared that a woman was sad because she and her best friend had an unresolved conflict from over a decade ago. Because so much time had passed, both parties perceived the conflict to be insurmountable. The chasm between the two was thought to be too large. After thinking and praying about the conflict, the woman decided to take one small step and ask her friend if they could talk. This was a risk, but the woman made the first effort to re-claim their friendship. The other woman was grateful and relieved that her friend made the initial effort. Through lots of tears and honest communication, the conflict was resolved and they are working on re-building their friendship.

The average amount of money saved for retirement by baby boomers (age 50) is $20,000. This statistic is amazing because if a person from this age-group works to age 65, he or she only have a short period of time left to earn money in which to save for the future. Obviously, most people from this era did not save a little from each paycheck. Many who lived through the Great Depression learned the discipline of saving money and the greatness of compound interest. Many children were taught at an early age (much to their youthful chagrin), that you "pay yourself first"—save a proportion of your earnings. Even though initially the interest income might be small, after forty years it adds up to a large amount.

On a daily basis, you might think you have a "great oak" that is too big to cut down. For example, your entire house might be a mess. Instead of shutting down and doing nothing, decide to clean one room. You might have pictures of your children from the past five years in a box. Instead of putting off the scrapbook project, first sort the pictures into years. You haven't exercised in months and you feel it's too late to start again. No, make a "little stroke" and walk around the block. You might have gained some weight over the years. Don't make an unrealistic goal, but cut out desserts for a while. You attempt to meditate for fifteen minutes, but your mind races from one thought to another. Persevere and incrementally your mind will slow down.

The explorer, David Livingstone said, "I am prepared to go anywhere, provided it be forward." Start today with little strokes that will help you cut down problems in your life. You will move yourself forward into a bigger life.

Today, I will name a "great oak" in my life that needs to be resolved. Specifically, I will _____.

Today, I will make the initial step of resolving the problem by _____.

Today, I will call an old friend or relative who has drifted away. Specifically, I will _____.

Today, I will start the process of moving forward. Specifically, I will _____.

Today, I will save a little bit more, so there will be a larger pot of gold at the end. Specifically, I will _____.

Today, I will move forward—one step at a time. Specifically, I will _____.

Today, I will _____.

Chapter Thirty-Four
Mind-*Body*-Spirit

The tongue weighs practically nothing, but few can hold it.

"I'm not one to gossip, but I have to tell you…"
"You can't believe what I just heard…"
"I feel bad to tell you this, but…"

John Dryden, an 17th century English poet, dramatist and critic, believed that people "…think too little, and talk too much." Most of us are guilty of this. We gossip, pass on juicy news, and even share hurtful information. This is a side of our humanity that is quite dark.

Most of us are not consciously mean-spirited. But we do have habits that are not healthy. Gossiping and not holding our tongue are habits—and habits are difficult to break. By acknowledging that language is a double-edged sword and our tendency to use both sides of the sword, we can practice a more sacred manner of communicating.

We have been given the gift of language. "If the tongue had not been framed for articulation, man would still be a beast in the forest," Ralph Waldo Emerson eloquently penned. This gift obviously can be used in helpful and harmful ways. We can use language to help others, communicate needs, share emotions, and create a healthy community. We can also use language to tear down others, build walls, and spread negativity. Proverbs 12:18, captures the different ways in which we can use this gift: "Rash words are like sword thrusts, but the tongue of the wise brings healing."

An ancient Chinese proverb states, "When words reach the tip of your tongue, hold back half of them." It takes great discipline and wisdom to know what to say and what to hold back. Usually the adage that most of our mothers taught us is the greatest barometer: "If you don't have something nice to say, don't say it at all."

"The words of the tongue should have three gatekeepers," is a wonderful Arab proverb that speaks to this paradox. Each gatekeeper is an internal awareness and discernment of what we are about to speak. The first gatekeeper must ask, "Is this true?" This question will sometimes stop our tongue from wagging. If we do not directly hear the information from the source, we don't know for certain that what we're hearing is true. The second gatekeeper asks, "Is it kind?" This question gets to our motivation: are we responding from the heart and desire to be helpful or are we responding from old hurts and about to use cutting words. The last gatekeeper asks, "Is it necessary?" If our internal awareness is focused on being compassionate, loving, and helpful, many words we are about to share will be censored. Utilizing the three gatekeepers will keep our spoken words to being truthful, kind and functional.

There is a poignant story of a woman who gossiped and said many untrue things about others. She was confronted about her behavior, but she did not stop spreading unkind things about others. One day, an elder from the village gave her a task to perform. She was to take a bag of feathers and place a feather in each yard of the village.

She did the task and then returned to the elder. He said, "You are to return to each home and retrieve the feathers." She frowned and said that this would be impossible because they would have blown away. She stopped and then realized the point the elder was trying to make. The unkind things we say cannot be taken back. It was an insight that changed her life.

Always keep your words soft and sweet, just in case you have to eat them. Hesiod, an 8th century B.C. Greek poet wrote, "A sparing tongue is the greatest treasure among men." Let us all build upon this treasure and all of our lives will be bigger.

Today, I will be aware of my propensity to gossip by _____.

Today, I will consciously not pass on "juicy" news by _____.

Today, I will think before I talk by _____.

Today, I will further live the adage, "If I don't have something nice to say, I won't say anything at all" by _____.

Today, I will honor the gift of language and speak in healthy ways by _____.

Today, I will be strong and hold my tongue by _____.

Today, I will _____.

Chapter Thirty-Five
Mind-Body-*Spirit*

In giving you receive.

Do you remember the time you helped someone and then felt really good afterwards? In giving assistance you received joy and a sense of goodness. It didn't have to be a big, grand act. Sharing a smile or letting a car merge into your lane creates a good feeling.

The negative side is also true with this paradox. If you give out anger, you will receive back hostility or resentment. If you live out of fear, you will receive back negative thoughts and act in an unhealthy manner. A Chinese proverb states, "The fire you kindle for your enemy often burns yourself more than him."

Every action we take is like dropping a rock in a pond. It creates ripples that affect the pond. Once the ripples reach the shore, they move back to the source. If we create ripples of goodness, goodness comes back. If we create negative ripples, negativity will return and our life becomes small, unhappy, and miserable.

There is a challenging story that gives a picture of what heaven and hell are like. In hell, every one is at a banquet table with wonderful, delicious food in front of them. Their forks and spoons are very long—so long that they can't turn them to their mouth and feed themselves. So the people in hell have pleasurable food in front of them, but they are starved throughout eternity.

In heaven, the people are also sitting at a banquet table with delicious food. Their forks and spoons are also so long that they can't feed themselves. But the folks in heaven use their eating utensils to feed the people across from them. They actually give the food to each other. This way, everyone is nourished and has a heavenly experience.

Chuang Tzu, a Taoist philosopher of ancient China, spoke to the truth of this parable when he said: "Theirs was the fullness of heaven and earth; the more that they gave to others, the more they had."

The Christian adage "as you sow, so shall ye reap" and the Buddhist concept of karma both speak of this paradox. Karma is a force generated by a person's actions and thoughts. Every word, notion, and deed has an effect on others and one's self. Karma is a wind that is always blowing. It all depends on how you set your sails. Hoarding, gossiping, or foul moods will move us to a "hellish" port. Kind words and compassion will guide us to a "heavenly" port.

The problems in life come when we're sowing one thing and expecting to reap something entirely different. An interesting and unique definition of neurosis is when a person is doing something that doesn't work and he does the behavior even more strongly expecting to create a different result. If you find yourself in a hole that you want to get out of, the number one rule is to stop digging!

A fun practice is to place six marbles in a pocket of your clothing at the beginning of the day. Your goal is to say six kind words, and/or perform six kind acts per day. After each kind action, move a marble from one pocket to another. By the end of the day, all marbles need to be in the other pocket.

Another practice is to make every day a new type of gift exchange—you give and you will receive. This idea is similar to practicing random acts of kindness. Why has this exercise become so popular? It creates a win-win situation. Obviously we are helping another person, and we are helping our selves because it feels good to do good.

The truth of the matter is it's your choice. Do you want a small life or a big life? Be aware of what you give out, because you will receive it back.

Today, I will give out love by _____.
Today, I will give out peace by _____.
Today, I will give out forgiveness by _____.
Today, I will practice a random act of kindness by _____.
Today, I will "feed" another person by _____.
Today, I will share my strengths and talents by _____.
Today, I will _____.

Chapter Thirty-Six
Mind-Body-*Spirit*

If you want to hang on, you need to let go.

This paradox deals with control, which is probably the biggest issue that keeps us stuck in life. Control is fear-based and takes many forms:

We hold on to what we know—even if it is not good for us—because we know it. This is fear of the unknown and trying to control our environment.

We say, "I know what is best for my kids and they will do as I say." This is trying to control another person.

We say, "The Universe needs to be changed and I am the one to do it." This is trying to control everyone and everything.

As young people we need to learn how to control our lives. It is necessary to learn how to grow out of diapers, eat healthy things before dessert (delay gratification), or say no to strangers. Teens want even more control in their lives and strive for independence. They need to learn healthy coping skills and how to make good decisions when they're given more privileges. An adolescent can now drive a car, and, metaphorically, he wants to drive his own "car of life." It is normal for his parents to be in the "passenger seat" watching how he's doing. If the teen continues to make good decisions and stay off the "shoulder of the road" or the "ditch," his parents don't have to "hit the brakes" or "grab the steering wheel." The teen will earn more freedoms and be in greater control of his life.

As we move into adulthood, this great strength of control can become a weakness (Paradox Thirty). We are then like the monkey in the jungle who is so easily hunted by simply chaining a banana stalk to a tree. The monkey grabs the banana stalk fiercely, trying to wrestle it away, screaming as he hears the hunters approach, bellowing as he is slain. The monkey never realizes that to simply let go might lead to freedom and safety.

We get so good at controlling our lives we start trying to control other peoples' lives. We think we know what is best for our children. Or we think we know the best solution to our neighbor's problem. The Alcoholics Anonymous and Al-Anon traditions speak to this issue. Al-Anon's *Courage to Change* says in part: "I must learn to give those I love the right to make their own mistakes and recognize them as theirs alone."

We think we control our lives so well that we don't include God in our daily lives. If we don't move out of trying to overly control our lives and others, we'll never fully see how the Spirit can help us on our journey. Letting go is a process: we let go and then we grab for control. Later, we might let go for a longer period of time before we grab on again. With practice, we can let go more than we grab the "banana stalk." This is not a one-time practice—it is on-going.

We have a tendency to do a poor job of letting go, forgiving and healing old hurts and conflicts. Our ego wants us to maintain the identity of victim, and hold on to our woundedness. The spiritual practice of forgiveness and "turning the other cheek" is a foreign concept to many of us. Two of Ann Landers often quoted "Gems" from her readers speak wisely this: "Hanging onto resentment is letting someone you despise live rent-free in your head," and "Hatred is like acid. It does more harm to the container in which it is stored than to the object on which it is poured."

Thinking we can totally control our life keeps us in a small box. Hanging on to old wounds and conflicts keeps us in a small box. There is great freedom, goodness, and knowledge outside our box.

If you continue to try and control life and not allow God to be the Chief Navigator of your metaphorical car, the odds are high you will end up on the wrong road or on a dead end.

If you want to soar, let God sit in the navigator's seat while you drive. Trust. Then trust some more. True, there will probably be some turbulence. But are you really happy with your present path? Eventually you find out that the team of God and you can make more of your life than you can alone.

Today, I will let go of my preconceived ways of doing
  things by _____.
Today, I will let go of an expectation of my kids
  that is causing problems in our relationships by

  _____.
Today, I will let go of an expectation of my spouse
  or partner that is causing problems in our
  relationship by _____.
Today, I will let go of my desire to change others by

  _____.
Today, I will be responsible, yet non-attached to
  outcomes by _____.
Today, I will ask God to be with me on my journey by

  _____.
Today, I will _____.

Chapter Thirty-Seven
Mind-Body-*Spirit*

God writes straight with crooked lines.

God is the Alpha and the Omega, the Ultimate Creator of our universe. Divine laws govern this incredible creation. They are found in the many different religions. Judeo-Christian belief systems have the Ten Commandments; Buddhism describes the Four Noble Truths; the Toltec masters wrote about the Four Agreements. God's universal truths give us straight and direct access to a life full of love, joy, and acceptance.

God also granted humans the gift of free will thereby making us co-creators. It is an honor that God empowered us to further create the universe and to co-create our lives. Free will is not all good or all bad. Free will has both negative *and* positive influences. (Another example of "both-and" thinking instead of "either-or" thinking.) Free will can take us down wandering and crooked roads.

God gave us the opportunity—even the right—to make decisions for ourselves. A great example of this is the parable of the prodigal son. In this story, the son asks his father for his share of the inheritance. His father freely gives it to him, just as God freely gives us our inheritance of gifts and talents. As we make decisions with the use of the inheritance we have the responsibility to deal with the natural consequences of these decisions. The prodigal son had to deal with the end result of his choices—the crooked line of his journey. He returned home and was fully accepted by his father—as God accepts us after our waywardness. The older brother, who never left on his own "crooked road," does not know his father or understand his ways.

Do you remember reading *The Odyssey* by Homer in high school or college? It is the story of Odysseus and his twenty-year travel back home after the Trojan War. Odysseus's journey was not a straight line back home to his wife Penelope and his son Telemachus. Odysseus was side lined by the Lotus Eaters, Cyclops, the Keeper of the Winds, Giants, enchantress Circe, the land of Death, the Sirens, Charybdis, and many other problems and difficulties. Only by Odysseus's resolve, hard work, and praying to his Gods, did he finally return home and save his wife and son from the suitors.

We are much like Odysseus. We are capable of making healthy *and* unhealthy choices, and being distracted off course. Like Odysseus, we need to take responsibility for our actions, and daily ask for God's help and guidance. We need to be less controlling and ask for divine assistance. If we are trying to align ourselves with God's will, our journeys will be less crooked.

If we do not blame but instead take responsibility for our actions and look for the messages within the failure, sooner than later we will get back on the road to success. (If we learn our lesson, maybe we will even be grateful and find the benefit of our crooked road.) If not, we will have to come back the same crooked road (Paradox Forty) until we learn our lesson.

The football great Sam Rutigliano said: "A man can make mistakes, but he isn't a failure until he starts blaming someone else." Other people will try and affect our decisions and further create "crooked lines." They will throw out bait to see if they can get us to follow their path. English poet John Dryden wrote, "Better shun the bait than struggle in the snare." Also, our humanness will create "crooked lines" because of our shortsighted vision or egocentric ideas. We need to be aware of both others and our self in order to straighten out our crooked lines.

Most people love to be on the top of the mountain. The view is breathtaking and mountain-top experiences are exhilarating. However, when one is up that high, the oxygen level is too low and there is very limited opportunity for vegetation growth. Most of the growth is down in the valleys. The pain and suffering of the valley motivates one to learn one's lesson, learn perseverance, more fully trust God, and climb to higher destinations. Life is big. Embrace the mountaintops *and* the valleys. Take a risk. If your journey goes a little crooked, keep the faith and change directions. You will create a bigger life.

Today, I will listen to the will of God for my life by _____.

Today, I will learn from my mistakes and get back on the road by _____.

Today, I will take responsibility for my life by _____.

Today, I will try to create a straighter line to God's will for my life by ____.

Today, I will pray to God for guidance in my life by _____.

Today, I will not give in to the Sirens, Lotus Eaters, and Keeper of the Winds by _____.

Today, I will _____.

Chapter Thirty-Eight
Mind-Body-*Spirit*

"Your children are not your children."
Kahil Gibran

Children are one of the greatest gifts from God. God has personally given us custody of a few of his creations.

Job 31:15 states, "God made me in my mother's womb." The painter Pollack said, "Babies are living jewels, dropped unstained from heaven."

Most of us believe these statements initially, but we slowly tend to take back the ownership. We start to "own" our children. Their successes are our successes. Their failings are our failings. Our children become an extension of us. This occurs because of a process called projection. Projection is attributing an attitude or behavior to another. It is a thinking process that twists perception to "we do not see things as they are, but we see things as we are." We "create" the world we see. For example, many fathers want their sons to be successful in sports in which they participated. If the father wasn't overly successful in his sport of choice, he will sign his son up for that sport, talk to him about the importance of that sport, and push him to be successful. Now the son can live out those unmet dreams. Many mothers want their daughters to participate in activities like cheerleading or dance that are more culturally rewarded. They project the importance of these activities onto their daughters. They drive the daughters to practices, buy them outfits at very early ages, and verbally and nonverbally reinforce the importance of that activity. A mother in Texas went so far to kill another cheerleader so her daughter would make the squad.

We forget that our children came through us, but they are not of us. Once we try to live through them and "own" their successes and failures, harm is done to all parties involved. We will inadvertently create smaller lives for our children.

We need to continually remind ourselves that our children are not our children. Yes, we are supposed to be responsible and teach them our values and beliefs. Yes, we are supposed to help them find their gifts and nurture them. That is what one does when one accepts custody of someone else's possession.

When parents aren't attached to any outcomes, they will be less likely to project their wants and unmet desires onto their children. They will see more clearly what the innate gifts and talents are of their children. Their son might come into the world with a gift of music. Their daughter might want to play a sport and not be on the sideline cheering on the team. Parents will be more likely to honor their children's unique talents when they don't see them as extensions of themselves, but gifts from God with their own personality and life mission.

Charles Dickens, the great English author wrote this very endearing thought, "I love these little people; and it is not a slight thing, when they, who are so fresh from God, love us."

The beauty of this paradox is if we fully live it, we will be better parents and happier human beings. We will make a bigger world for our children.

Today, I will give my children back to God.

Today, I will give glory to God by being a responsible parent.

Today, I will practice loving my children ... because they are one of the greatest gifts from God.

Today, I will not make my children fit into my personality mold.

Today, I will take off my blinders and truly see the talents of my children and help nurture their God-given gifts.

Today, I will gently nudge my children, but not push them.

Today, I will _____.

Chapter Thirty-Nine
Mind-Body-*Spirit*

You get what you give.

A ten year old sees his mother's joy when she receives a letter. The child wants to be happy like mom and states that he also wants to get letters. She tells him, "If you want to receive letters, you must send letters."

The child fights this truth because he wants the benefit of a one-way street. He doesn't want to spend the time to write, but he sure wants the letters.

This mother's advice is a truth throughout life. If you want friends, you have to be friendly. If you want to receive respect, you have to give respect. If you find yourself being loved by a limited number of people, you are giving love in a very limited manner.

Admiral James B. Stockdale, a one-time vice presidential candidate said, "…What we need for leaders are men of heart who are so helpful that they, in effect, do away with the need of their jobs. But leaders are never out of a job, never out of followers. Strange as it sounds, great leaders gain authority by giving it away." William A. White, an author who ran for governor of Kansas because of his opposition to the Klu Klux Klan, stated another example of this paradox: "Liberty is the one thing you can't have unless you give it to others."

The law of reciprocity states that there is a natural flow to the universe. Since everything is interrelated and connected, you will receive back what you send out. All major religions speak to this truth. T'ai Shang Kan Ying Pien stated this Taoist belief: "Regard your neighbor's gain as your own gain, and your neighbor's loss as your own loss." Leviticus 19:18 in the Old Testament states: "...thou shalt love thy neighbor as yourself." The Jewish Talmud states: "What is hateful to you, do not to your fellow man. This is the law, all the rest is commentary." 2 Corinthians 9:6-8 in the New Testament states: "Whoever sows sparingly will also reap sparingly, and whoever sows generously will also reap generously." Black Elk, the famous Medicine Man of the Oglala Sioux said, "All things are our relatives, what we do to everything, we do to ourselves. All is really one."

This natural flow applies to all aspects of our lives. For example, money and possessions are not stagnant, but dynamics of life. Financially contributing to worthy causes or passing on goods, will create an open flow of financial energy. So, paradoxically, if you want more money, you need to give away more money.

This paradox is powerful in respect to relationships

with others. If you feel your life partner is being distant and unfeeling, give him or her the intimacy that you want. Give her something that is important to her—make a special meal, get a baby sitter, or rub her shoulders. Make sure your motivation is sincere and not manipulative. In time, living this paradox will create a full circle of giving and receiving.

Quid pro quo (something for something) giving is a mentality that will harm the beauty of helping others and inevitably stop the natural flow of the law of reciprocity. The motivation for "tit for tat" giving is selfish and self-centered. These mind-sets are like a black hole which never can be fulfilled. Awareness of the motivation of your giving is of the utmost importance.

The illusion of scarcity can stop us from living this truth. Sometimes we buy into the concept that love is scarce, friendships are scarce, and money is scarce. The truth is that God created our universe in a plentiful manner. God wants a plentiful life for all of us. God and the potential of the Creative Force is not limited by our thinking. Please do not allow yourself to be limited. Do not diminish the natural flow of life to you. This would create too small of a small life. There is a big life for you to live.

Today, I will "sow generously" by _____.
Today, I will give more of what I want from life by

_____.

Today, I will further accept the truth that the Universe is not scarce by _____.

Today, I will more fully trust that God wants a full and plentiful life for me. Specifically, I will _____

Today, I will quit hoarding clothes, money, time, and love, and share them freely with others. Specifically, I will _____.

Today, I will be more aware of my motivation behind my giving by _____.

Today, I will _____.

Chapter Forty
Mind-Body-*Spirit*

The road you leave behind is the same road you are going to have to come back down.

Life is full of lessons. We are in a huge schoolhouse we call earth. If we do not learn our lessons now, they <u>will</u> come back to us. Life will bring them benevolently back to us for our benefit.

This truth will help us when a difficult situation crosses our path. The path of least resistance—ignoring and hoping it will go away—will only delay the inevitable. The famous first sentence in *The Road Less Traveled* states, "Life is difficult." M. Scott Peck based this statement on the first of the Four Noble Truths of Buddhism, which is "Life is suffering." Peck goes on to say, "This is a great truth...because once we truly see this truth, we transcend it."

When one has to "come back down" the same road

to learn a life lesson, it usually is more difficult. A normal response is to judge and blame the "road" and try to leave it. Wanting to escape will never work because our own fears, painful histories, and self-imposed limits will follow us. The Universe will bring us down the road again because our soul needs to learn that specific lesson. We cannot escape the truth that what is refused will continue to return. For example, if a man is consistently having difficult times in relationships with women, he probably doesn't need to find yet another woman to date; he should learn the specific lesson of communication, intimacy, or trust.

In 1824, Walter Savage Landor wrote in *Imaginary Conversations of Literary Men and Statesmen*, "There is no easy path leading out of life, and few are the easy ones that lie within it." To transcend life's difficulties requires commitment, work, and practice. If we accept the lessons, and know that they are for our benefit, it will help us embrace this mindset and be more successful in life. Remember—the only place where success precedes work is in the dictionary.

There are many processes by which we learn our life lessons. One strategy is a rhyming method: name it, claim it, which will allow you to tame it, to ultimately reframe it. By first *naming* the lesson, we know what exactly we need to work on. Then *claiming* the lesson allows us to own it and not project it onto someone else. *Taming* will naturally occur by practicing new ways of thinking and acting. And then we can *reframe* it to new behaviors and an overall healthier lifestyle.

In the 1993 movie *Groundhog Day*, Bill Murray

plays a weatherman who is very unhappy about an assignment. He does not treat others nicely and tries to use them for his benefit. When he awakens in the morning, he realizes it is Groundhog Day again. Because he is not learning his life lesson of treating others with love and respect he continues to live the tag line of the movie: "He's having the worst day of his life...over, and over..." Once he embraces the lesson, he finally gets to leave that road behind.

In the Star Wars movie *The Empire Strikes Back,* Luke Skywalker is attempting to use the Force to lift a starfighter craft out of the swamp. Skywalker becomes very frustrated and tells Yoda that he's trying to do it. Yoda responds, "Do or do not. There is no try." This is similar to when Jesus told his followers not to be just hearers of the words, but to be doers. The spiritual road to new frontiers is not about trying. It's all about doing the practices.

Albert Einstein defined insanity as, "Doing the same thing over and over and expecting different results." When you are stuck, you need to do something different so you can learn your life lessons. This will allow yourself to travel many new roads so you can see the beauty of this big, incredible schoolhouse.

Today, I will embrace the road I am on by _____.
Today, I will name the lesson that is this road by __.
Today, I will start the process of learning that lesson
    by _____.
Today, I will not fight my lessons by _____.
Today, I will admit that life is difficult so I can start to
    transcend the suffering in my life by _____.

Today, I will not judge or blame another, and I will try to own the part of the lesson that is mine by _____.

Today, I will _____.

Chapter Forty-One
Mind-Body-*Spirit*

The way to heaven is through hell.

We have all left the Garden of Eden. We have "fallen" because of our humanness. We have taken on things from our parents' humanness, our friends' humanness, and the humanness of everyone who has crossed our path.

It is very difficult to heal these parts of our humanity. It is very difficult to admit we are jealous or greedy, that we feel hatred, and anger. It is very difficult to go through the pain and travel back to the paradise of the Garden of Eden within us. In the inner paradise, we reconcile that the kingdom of God lives within us.

The way back to a heavenly state is to admit that we have these "hells" inside of us and to embrace them. We have to admit that our anger toward another person has less to do with them and more to do with us. United States Supreme Court Justice Louis Brandeis said that "sunlight is the best disinfectant." It is hard to travel through the "hell" of admitting that our partner, spouse, or friend is right when they point out a problem area in our life. It's difficult to put the "disinfectant" on our wound. And it is the best healer and springboard to personal growth.

Carl Jung referred to these places as our shadow. These are parts of ourselves that we don't like to admit are part of us. Examples are unresolved issues with a parent, or feelings of jealousy, resentment, or rage. The shadow is anything that goes against the projected image of our public self. If we look at these issues, and bring light to them, the shadow will be reduced and lose its power. Jung went on to say, "One does not become enlightened by imagining figures of light, but by making the darkness conscious."

A Native American legend tells about a conversation between a snake and a lizard. The snake asks the lizard how he gets to the shady spots before him. The lizard responds by saying, "You seek the shade and I seek the shadow." For the Native Americans, the lizard medicine is for building strength by working through one's areas of resistance and fears. If this difficult work is done, the person will ultimately find a nice "shady spot" of respite.

When most people are confronted with a problem, they don't want any "hell" options—they only want "heaven" choices. That is not how life works on this earth-plane. By going through the "hell," the problems can become an opportunity for growth. M. Scott Peck writes in *The Road Less Traveled*, "Delaying gratification is a process of scheduling the pain and pleasure of life in such a way as to enhance the pleasure by meeting and experiencing the pain first and getting it over with. It is the only decent way to live."

Robert Frost wrote, "The best way out is always through." Accepting our human shortcomings, healing our hurts and sorrows, are examples of traveling through "hell" and into our shadow. These torments and traumas are the entrance gate, testing our sincerity and our commitment to the journey. A healthy way to honor this process is to thank God and acknowledge that adversity is for one's own good and growth—even though you do not know specifically what that is.

Paul wrote to the Thessalonians, "Give thanks in all circumstances." He did not write to give thanks for all circumstances. For examples, if I get into a car accident, it would be silly to be thankful *for* the accident. But I will practice being thankful *in* the circumstance that no one got hurt, and insurance will help pay for the repairs. This practice of having a grateful attitude is the only way back to heaven on earth—the only way to live the big life for which you were created.

Today, I will own my human shortcomings by _____.
Today, I will be strong and see my shadow side by

_____.

Today, I will live more in the light by _____.
Today, I will give less power to the shadow issues by

_____.

Today, I will start the journey through a "hell" so to reach a more "heavenly" state by _____.

Today, I will gather the strength to start my travel back to the Garden of Eden within myself by _____.

Today, I will _____.

Chapter Forty-Two
Mind-Body-**Spirit**

In living life we sometimes forget to live.

In our efforts to make a living, raise a family, or keep up with the Joneses, we sometimes busy ourselves so much that we forget to truly live. This busyness can create a hollow shell that is devoid of the essence of life.

We have the propensity to hang on to old grudges or memories. This keeps us in the past and hinders us from enjoying today. We also worry about the future or plan so much for the future that we forget about today...which is the only place we can truly live. Our lives can only be lived right here and right now. We need to quit spending so much time in the past or the future. The present can really be a present.

In the movie *Dead Poets Society*, Robin Williams' character is a teacher in an all-boys prep school. Most of the young men come from affluent homes and their parents reinforce the values of pursuing only the "right" careers that will pay them lots of money and give them prestige. Williams' character knows the boys need to be stretched outside these cultural mores. He walks them out of the classroom to the hallway where pictures of alumni are hanging. Since all these alumni are dead, he reminds the students, "they are fertilizing daffodils" and "we are food for worms." He then has a student read from a Walt Whitman poem. "Gather ye rosebuds while ye may, old time is still aflying, and this same flower that smiles today, tomorrow will be dying." Williams' character then challenges the students to make their lives extraordinary. He uses the Latin phrase that is now on bumper stickers, T-shirts, and garden rocks: "carpe diem—seize the day."

John Tarrant poetically writes in *The Light Inside the Dark* (another paradox), about the beauty and power of our existence: "Life has seduced us and we shall, no doubt, die of this seduction. Yet it is marvelous too, and if we do not let ourselves be seduced by existence, there is nowhere for the fingers of eternity to seize us."

Live fully in whatever you do. Take a different route to work and notice your surroundings. Take a walk and be aware of each step. Plant a garden and feel the dirt between your fingers. Re-connect with a hobby. Smile at a stranger. The results will be experiences more full of life.

This poem speaks simply and deeply about this paradox:

"This is the beginning of a new day.

God has given me this day to use as I will.
I can waste it or grow in its light and be of service to others.
But what I do with this day is important because I have exchanged a day of my life for it.
When tomorrow comes,
Today will be gone forever.
I will not regret the price I have paid for it."

Novelist and diarist Anais Nin wrote, "And the day came when the risk it took to remain tightly closed in a bud was more painful than the risk it took to bloom." We all have a tendency to hang on to what we know and to create habits. We do today, what we did the day before, and the day before that. These habits give us the illusion that we are safe. These habits also create a "closed bud" which does not allow our natural talents and abilities to unfold. If we find ourselves living a small life, it is time to take a calculated risk and allow ourselves to "bloom" into a bigger life.

Today, I will live more fully by _____.
Today, wherever I am, I will be present to that situation by _____.
Today, I will more fully realize that "now" is the only time I have to live by _____.
Today, I will seize the day by _____.
Today, I will pick up my life that I have put aside, and start to really live by _____.
Today, I will realize that the present moment is a present to me by _____.
Today, I will _____.

Chapter Forty-Three
Mind-Body-*Spirit*

The soulful path involves discovering our "higher" selves while exploring our "depths."

Psychologist Carl Jung coined the term "shadow" to describe the parts of ourselves we don't like to admit are within us. We have a tendency to deny their existence and push the shadow side deep down into our unconscious. We feel if we allow these "negative" traits to enter our awareness, they will overpower us, or we will act them out. Paradoxically, if we bring to light these traits, they will lose power because we can make more conscious decisions.

Children are scared at bedtime because monsters are "living" in the closet or under the bed. The monsters have more power in the dark. When we turn on the lights, the fears that once were in the shadows are de-powered.

When one finds shadow issues while exploring one's depths, it is very important to claim and honor what is found. If one doesn't own the issue, he will stay stuck and not be able to grow into his "higher" self. The Chinese have a saying that describes this process: "huang tang bu huang yao"—changing the water that has been soaked with herbs, not the herb itself. The message is to deal with the problem or issue—let go of the crisis or trait that you no longer need—or else it will continue to permeate your existence.

There are personality traits that children have that their parents or culture have not reinforced. As young children, they might have been taught that those traits were wrong and they unconsciously shoved them down into a level of unawareness. Now, as adults, they can retrieve these lost characteristics and interests and move into a lifestyle more true to their selves (Paradox Forty-eight). For example, an introverted child who naturally receives energy from internal experiences is pushed by extroverted parents to join clubs, invite friends over, or join team sports. She rarely gets re-energized and wonders what is wrong with her self. Another example is a young boy who likes music but does not like sports. His father pushes him into athletic events. The boy tries to please his dad, constantly falls short, and ends up with low self-esteem.

God gave the Ten Commandments to Moses to share with everyone. All humans are capable of doing what the laws forbid in the "Thou shalt nots," and capable of obeying the laws of the "Thou shalts." For example, if an unhappy middle aged man doesn't shine a light on his unfulfilling sex life, he might act out in an adulterous way. On the other side of the coin, if a woman doesn't love herself, she might believe she can't "love your neighbor as yourself." If she looked deep inside to see the root of her low self-esteem, it is probable she will more fully love her neighbor. If we explore the depths of *all* of our humanness, shine light on our shadows, we can then grow and evolve into a "higher" self of wisdom and spiritual practices.

The Christian religion calls us to become "Christ-like." Jesus told us the kingdom of God is within. Buddha challenged everyone to find his or her "Buddha nature." Mother Teresa stated, "We must become holy, not because we want to feel holy, but because Christ must be able to live his life fully in us." Likewise, Ralph Waldo Emerson wrote, "What lies behind us and what lies before us are tiny matters compared to what lies within us." These are examples of discovering one's "higher self."

John Ruskin, a great British art critic and social commentator of the Victorian Era said: "The highest reward for man's toil is not what he gets for it, but what he becomes by it." By exploring your depths and discovering your higher self, you will live a big life.

Today, I will open myself to exploring the depths of my humanness by _____.

Today, I will bring to the light one "unfavorable" trait I see in myself. Specifically, I will _____ _____.

Today, I will continue my journey through the depths to the higher level of existence by _____.

Today, I will be careful not to "push down" a shadow trait but leave it in the light so I can work through it. Specifically, I will _____.

Today, I will let go of old baggage that has weighed me down. Specifically, I will _____.

Today, I will climb to the heights in which I am capable. Specifically, I will _____.

Today, I will _____.

Chapter Forty-Four
Mind-Body-*Spirit*

"If you want to kiss the sky, better learn
how to kneel."

U2

Within our human nature is the desire to transcend our humanness. There is a blissful feeling when we relax our ego boundaries and feel connected to the "Greater Good."

One of the best ways to reach those heights is to kneel down, pray, and meditate. This process helps us to acknowledge a Higher Power, helps us to realize that we don't stand alone, and to accept our interconnectedness.

Our problems then seem less important. It is easier to let go (Paradox Thirty-six) of life's uncertainties, trust, and rise above to a more joyful existence. Josephine Baker, civil rights activist and the first woman of African descent to star in a modern major motion picture said, "I believe in prayer. It's the best way we have to draw strength from heaven."

If you want a spiritual awakening, accept the fact that you cannot do it alone. *And* solitary disciplines like prayer, meditation, quiet time, journaling, yoga or any other discipline that gets you out of yourself (Paradox Seventeen) and into your True Self will help your spiritual growth. Mahatma Gandhi said, "Prayer is not asking. It is a longing of the soul. It is daily admission of one's weakness. It is better in prayer to have a heart without words than words without a heart." American Baptist minister Martin Luther King Jr. said, "To be a Christian without prayer is no more possible than to be alive without breathing."

Andrew Newberg, a professor at the University of Pennsylvania, is a leading figure in the emerging science of neurotheology, which explores the links between spirituality and the brain. By scanning the brain, scientists have located a part that is responsible for differentiating between the physical self and the rest of existence.

He researched the neurophysiological correlates of meditation and how brain function is associated with mystical and religious experiences. Brain scans show what Christian mystics would call a "mystical union" with God or a Buddhist monk would call "interconnectiveness."

This suggests that when the ego-self is pushed aside during prayer and meditation, our "reality" moves toward unification with the Ultimate Source— as if we are kissing the heavenly skies.

Psychologist Abraham Maslow proposed a

hierarchy of needs based on the belief that humans are interested in growing and evolving. The first level is the physiological needs of food, shelter, oxygen, and water. The second level includes safety needs of an orderly, stable and predictable world. The third level is belonging and love needs. We seek intimate relationships and need to feel part of groups or associations. The fourth level is self-esteem needs— the drive for respect from other and self. The fifth and final level is self-actualization. There are two levels of self-actualizing people. The first is the people who are emotionally healthy. The second are Self-transcenders who are spiritual in their orientation. Their lives are based on prayer, joy, and service to others. They have "peak experiences," where they experience an expansion of self and also a sense of unity and meaningfulness of life. In other words, they are "kissing the sky," because they know "how to kneel." They live big lives.

Today, I will practice letting go of an uncertainty by _____.

Today, I will set aside 15 minutes of quiet time in the morning. Specifically, I will _____.

Today, I will talk to God more often than yesterday. Specifically, I will _____.

Today, I will realize that I cannot do it alone and I am not alone by _____.

Today, I will start the process of learning how to meditate. Specifically, I will _____ _____.

Today, I will wake up earlier so I can take a quiet walk, journal, pray or meditate. Specifically, I will _____.

Today, I will _____.

Chapter Forty-Five
Mind-Body-*Spirit*

What hurts can also heal.

"Don't put that iodine on my cut!" the child yelled to his mom.

"I don't want my Band-Aid ripped off!" the little girl cried to her daddy.

"Don't pull that splinter out of my finger!" the boy said, fighting back tears.

We adults are a lot like children. We don't want to experience some short-term pain even though we know it would create some long-term gain.

Conflict is a normal part of being in a relationship. Most people are afraid of conflict, and haven't been shown how to resolve conflict, so they don't know the best ways to deal with it. Because of this, many relationships and groups are stuck in this hurtful stage. Talking about conflict with a friend is difficult. It is a risk to talk honestly about the hurt. You can begin by making "I" statements about your feelings and perceptions of the conflict. Talking through the problems can heal the friendship, and move the relationship to a better, more intimate and trusting place.

Looking at difficult or abusive past experiences can be hurtful. If we have repressed the old hurts, they tend to keep us mired and unhappy in our life. If we talk about the pain, and bring the experiences to light, this process can be very healing. It is a paradox that experiencing pain releases pain.

Singer and actress Reba McEntire said, "For me, singing sad songs often has a way of healing a situation. It gets the hurt out in the open into the light, out of the darkness."

This world we live in seems to be bipolar; the "good *and* the bad," the "yin *and* the yang," the "hurts *and* the pleasures." To live life in the most functional way, one has to embrace both poles. If we look at life as "either-or," which means we are trying to escape the negative and close our eyes to the "bad" side, the result will be a smaller life. Paradoxically, we will get stuck on the side we're tying to escape and then must endure the maladies that come with this state. However, if we embrace "both-and" (the hurts *and* pleasures); if we open our eyes to the full spectrum between the poles, we will grow and heal to a better place. Grammy nominated and Tony-winning singer, songwriter, and composer Duncan Sheik said, "I actually think sadness and darkness can be very beautiful and healing."

Theologian Martin Marty writes, "Brokenness and wounding do not occur in order to break human dignity but to open the heart so God can act." Similarly, Christian mystic Julian of Norwich stated, "Our wounds become the womb of wholeness." If we look honestly at our pain, the promise is that growth and healing will begin.

Mark Twain wrote, "I was born modest; not all over, but in spots." We all have "spots" where we hurt and are vulnerable. It's best not to deny these spots, because we can then turn our hurt into hurting others. If we acknowledge the spots to ourselves, we can turn pain into power, hurt into healing. The Persian poet Rumi wrote, "Through love all pain will turn to medicine."

Pain can be a gift, even if we usually do not want to receive it. If we accept and honor the gift of pain, we will usually get stronger, grow, and evolve into a closer relationship with our Higher Power. Mother Teresa said, "Suffering opens up space within that otherwise would not be there that God can come in and fill it." This team—God and you--will be creating a bigger life.

Today, I will acknowledge that part of the healing process can be painful by _____.

Today, I will seek a trusting relationship to help me get through the hurt by _____.

Today, I will practice seeing and living life as a "both-and" experience by _____.

Today, I will allow myself to get my feelings up and out (perhaps on paper) by _____.

Today, I will enter into a situation that might be painful short-term, but will probably be beneficial long-term by _____.

Today, I will make an appointment for a routine physical by _____.

Today, I will _____.

Chapter Forty-Six
Mind-Body-*Spirit*

"Work it in, to work it out."
Michael W. Smith

This lyric is from one of Michael W. Smith's contemporary Christian songs. The "it" in the first part of the quote refers to love.

Relationships are dynamic. Conflict is part of the experience and is inevitable in human interactions. For the relationship to grow and flourish, love is the ingredient needed to "work out" the conflict.

M. Scott Peck defines love as "The will to extend one's self for the purpose of nurturing one's own or another's spiritual growth." Hopefully, we see all of our endeavors and interactions: work, play, recreation, family, and friends as spiritual experiences and opportunities for spiritual growth. We don't have to like what people are doing, or even like the people.

But in order to transcend the conflict and see their divinity, we must "work in" love.

Our culture does not reinforce the inclusion of spirituality and love in all endeavors. In a pie diagram, one has the "slice" of work, family, friends, exercise, personal time, and spirituality. We are taught to balance those slices of the pie. With this paradigm, spiritual love is allocated to a certain slice. The truth is the entire "pie" is spiritual. *Everything* is sacred and worthy of the expression of love. Work love into all the "slices" of the pie. This practice will certainly work things out in a healthier manner.

The best map for this lifestyle is I Corinthians 13:4-7: "Love is patient, love is kind, love is not jealous or boastful; it is not arrogant or rude. Love does not insist on its own way; it is not irritable or resentful; it does not rejoice at wrong, but rejoices in the right. Love bears all things, believes all things, hopes all things, endures all things." Now, to move this truth from the abstract to the concrete, substitute your name whenever the word "love" or "it" appears. For example, "Pete is patient, Pete is kind; Pete is not jealous or boastful; Pete is not arrogant or rude..."

We tend to judge people who are different from us. Religious practices, cultural traditions, and sexual orientation are examples of differences that bring out our judgmental side. Martin Luther King Jr. said, "We must learn to live together as brothers or perish together as fools." Jesus stated it more strongly when he said we should love our enemy. Mahatma Gandhi said, "Whenever you are confronted with an opponent, conquer him with love." To break away from fear and move into love is the requisite for healthy relationships. Author Bertrand Russell wrote "To fear love is to fear life, and those who fear life are already three parts dead."

In 1967, Beatle John Lennon wrote a song from the Abbey Road Studio called "All You Need Is Love." The Allman Brothers Band wrote the song, "Love Is Everywhere." Many other songwriters remind us of the accessibility and power of love. Love is always present for us to help another person. It is our choice.

Gregory McNamee wrote in *Gila: The Life and Death of an American River*, "An anthropologist once asked a Hopi why so many of his people's songs were about rain. The Hopi replied that it was because water is so scarce. Is that why so many of your songs are about love?"

We are citizens of the world. In our little place in the world, let us live a big life and include love in our daily interactions and actions. Take a risk and extend yourself for the betterment of another. Work in love so to be fully alive...not "three parts dead."

Today, I will see my whole life as a spiritual experience by _____.

Today, I will work love into all my interactions by _____.

Today, I will embrace conflict and—with love—work out problems by _____.

Today, I will extend myself for the purpose of nurturing someone's spiritual growth by _____.

Today, I will practice seeing the divinity in each person by _____.

Today, I will work in love by _____.
Today, I will _____.

Chapter Forty-Seven
Mind-Body-*Spirit*

What we fear is really not there.

Being fearful of a wild animal, sudden loud noises, and a blazing fire comes from our evolutionary background. These are healthy fears and serve us well. There are many other fears that we create that undermine our relationship with God and our personal growth.

The Bible states three hundred and sixty-five times: "Fear not," or "Do not fear." The Talmud states, "Unhappy is he who mistakes the branch for the tree, the shadow for the substance."

We sometimes tend to think in fearful and narrow ways, which creates a small life of illusions and misperceptions. For example, some parents say, "My child is too shy. I'm afraid she will not have a good time in school." The parent is only looking at one characteristic of the child. In reality there is a well-adjusted, intelligent child who likes to read and play her musical instrument—and may be a bit shy.

Plato tells a story about humans who are all prisoners in a cave. We are bound and shackled and stand facing a wall of the cave, so that we can see only what is directly in front of us. Behind us puppets are being moved on their strings. Behind these figures is a fire that casts its light onto the puppets, projecting their shadows onto the wall. It is these shadows that we see; it is these shadows that we think are real.

Plato asks us to free ourselves from the shackles and turn around, so that we now face the fire. At first our eyes are so confused by the light that we see the puppets only dimly. But as our eyes grow more accustomed to the light, we begin to discern the puppets and then the fire, and know that we have only been looking at shadows. We are no longer prisoners of the cave. We are no longer prisoners to the puppeteer. We are free of fear. We *know* they were only illusions. We *know* they were products of our own mind.

We can then leave the cave and see life more clearly and truthfully. We can see that love permeates our existence. The universe is not scarce—in fact it is abundant.

Prayer is a helpful strategy in order that we may let go of fear. Prayer connects us to the goodness of God. Prayer can quiet our busy, fearful minds, and open the way for us to trust the infinite wisdom of God. The apostle John writes, "Perfect love casts out fear." This love comes from prayerfully giving our fears over to God, trusting, and finding something for which to be grateful. Success in ridding oneself of fear lies in making a deliberate choice to deal with the fear. Some people find this process to be easier by turning to their Higher Power.

In the movie *Star Wars*, the young hero, Luke Skywalker often became fearful and did not know what to do. Luke's mentor, Obi-Wan Kenobe, coached him to "Trust the Force." Obi-Wan's words moved Luke out of the fearful illusions his mind was creating, and towards the wisdom that comes from a Source greater than himself. We, too, need to find and create that trust.

Siddhartha Gautama, the Buddha, was trying to find the answer to the end of suffering. He was near starvation and sitting under the Bodhi tree when a young girl brought him a bowl of rice milk to restore his emaciated body. Mara, the Lord of Illusion, unleashed his armies—every death, fear, torment, and conceivable terror the mind could imagine. Siddhartha said, "O Mara, you cannot imprison me again. The rafters are broken, the ridgepole is sundered, I have seen the builder of the house."

Siddhartha was a man who saw clearly that fear is a product of the mind. He did not attach himself to any of Mara's illusions. He knew that there was no greater enemy than fear. After his awakening, he taught and modeled for forty-five years this and many other universal truths. Many people live happier and bigger lives by slaying fear, the enemy, and realizing it is an illusion.

Today, I will name a fear I am living by _____.

Today, I will face a fear and see its illusionary nature by _____.

Today, I will turn to the reality of love, trust and acceptance by _____.

Today, I will keep the faith, and also do the work that is mine to do by ____.

Today, I will "Trust the Force" by _____.

Today, I will not buy into a "shadow" that is projected onto my life by _____.

Today, I will _____.

Chapter Forty-Eight
Mind-Body-*Spirit*

We have sacrificed our self for our self-image.

Each and every one of us came into the world with our own unique talents, gifts, personality, and propensities. These God-given special traits create our true self.

Sadly, family members, peers, and society do not always honor these characteristics. For example, media sends thousands of messages that say we need to look and act certain ways. Our culture rewards achievement, extroversion, financial success, social positions, and certain professions. Madison Avenue says we need to wear fat ties, then thin ties. Bell bottoms, then capris. A preppy look, then a western look. These trends are endless, senseless, ceaseless, and externally driven.

Individually and collectively, we buy in to these

messages—usually at the expense of our true self. We can lose our caring and nurturing side and not pursue a teaching job because we think we need to climb the corporate ladder. We lose our connectiveness to nature because we think we have to be busy all the time. We lose touch with our soul because of our perceived need for external accomplishments. We lose our own integrity when we are afraid to resolve conflicts.

The process of trying to create a proper self-image is de-energizing. The target is always moving, it is expensive, and we continually worry if we are measuring up. The process of coming home to your true self can initially be scary, but it is a guarantee that you will be happier and more full of life.

The main developmental issue for adolescents is identity formation. It is typical for teens to try on many different identities. One week they may try to fit in with the athletic crowd, which will lead them to dress and talk a certain way. Then they might hang out with the drama crowd, which will create a new wardrobe and vocabulary. The main purpose of this experimentation is to find an identity that is a good fit. This process does not end in adolescence. The journey to our true self is life-long. Hopefully, we continue to shed the identities that no longer serve a good purpose and move toward the person God created.

Nathaniel Hawthorne wrote in *The Scarlet Letter,* "No man, for any considerable period, can wear one face to himself and another to the multitude, without finally getting bewildered as to which may be the true." When we get in a habit of wearing many masks, we become more comfortable with the habit instead of our true self. William Shakespeare wrote in *Hamlet,* "This above all, — to thine own self be true..."

Confucius said, "Cultivate the root. The leaves and branches will take care of themselves." One way to define the word "root" is our innate nature and how we came into the world. Is our "root" more of an introverted or extroverted nature? Is our "root" more mathematical or writing creative stories oriented? Does our "root" lead us to a more structured orderly lifestyle or a go with the flow lifestyle? If we look inward (Paradox Five) and honor our true self, we can let go of self-image concerns because we know the "leaves and branches will take care of themselves."

Martin Luther wrote, "We are not yet what we shall be, but we are growing toward it. The process is not finished but it is going on." This journey of letting go of self-image and honoring our true self will take time. God has a plan for each and every one of us. Flowing with Spirit and allowing our destiny to unfold, is the ultimate gift for our self and the Universe. It is a process of returning home to our true self and living a bigger life.

Today, I will be more aware of how my self-image is leading me.

Today, I will name a component of my self-image that I will let go.

Today, I will name a component of my true self that I will utilize.

Today, I will de-power the messages that come from Madison Avenue, media and culture.

Today, I will spend some quiet time remembering the activities that used to energize me.

Today, I will "try on" an identity that is closer to the true me.

Today, I will _____.

Chapter Forty-Nine
Mind-Body-*Spirit*

One can have peace amid the storm.

There are many "storms" in life. From bickering children to teenagers breaking curfew; early morning rush hour traffic to the boss making you work late; the long lines at the grocery store to short tempers from family members.

Just like the wind of the hurricane that destroys everything in its path, people who are in chaos want to destroy the serenity of others. There is a place—the eye of the hurricane—where destruction does not occur. In fact, it has been described as peaceful. How can we find this place in our day-to-day lives?

Many people tried to create storms in Jesus' life. He did not allow himself to get caught up in their chaos. Christ states in John 14:27: "Peace I leave with you, my peace I give to you, not as the world gives do I give to you." This promise works because it is spiritual truth—not earthly understanding.

Prayer and meditation help create peace amid the storms of life. The purpose of these practices is to quiet your mind, and help you get outside yourself, trust in something greater than you, and ask for assistance. Modern society stands for the opposite. We are taught to multi-task, trust only our selves, and be busy. This formula is the antithesis of peace. Living only these cultural norms is a stormy existence.

A common meditation practice is to be aware of your breath. This exercise simply asks you to be mindful of your breathing: breathe in and breathe out. Breathe in, breathe out. Focus on each breath and the gap between breaths. Soon, awareness will start to occur. You will notice that breathing in has a cooling sensation in your nostrils. Breathing out is warmer. Saying a mantra with each breath is also helpful. For example, stating out loud or to yourself, "Breathe in peace, breathe out negativity," will help you in many ways. First, physiologically, you will be slowing down your cardiovascular system. Instead of a rapid pulse, you will experience a calming throughout your body. Second, your mind will quit racing. It will slow down which will create a more peaceful existence. Third, if your mind is focused on spiritual and peaceful thoughts, automatically the chaotic, fearful, negative thoughts will subside.

One of the truths of life is that we cannot change other people. Even though, objectively, the other person might be creating chaos or treating you negatively, the only person you can change is you.

Creating your change to maintain inner peace can be practiced in many different ways. For example, the change could be not taking things personally. Another practice is letting negativity flow right past you. A typical religious practice is praying for the other person and loving them. Setting boundaries is a common counseling strategy. The important thread in all these practices is to not participate in the other person's storms. Mahatma Gandhi said, "Non-cooperation with evil is a sacred duty."

Along with keeping a safe distance from the chaos, acceptance of our reality is another beneficial strategy. A great example of this is Bobby Jones, one of the most gifted golfers in the history of the sport. Bobby had a rare and degenerative disease that ended his career and finally, his life. One of his most enduring and therapeutic messages came when he was asked about his disease. Bobby's response was, "We must play the ball as it lies." All of us have life situations that we probably would not have chosen. We can fight these realities and create more storms, or we can "play the ball as it lies," and find a more peaceful existence.

A silver haired woman was tired of the hatred and violence in the world. From 1953 to 1981, calling herself "Peace Pilgrim," she walked more than 25,000 miles on a personal pilgrimage for peace. She wrote, "The way of peace is the way of love. Love is the greatest power on earth. It conquers all things."

All of these practices try to create the same end result: maintaining peace amid the storms of life—which will create a bigger life.

Today, I will set aside at least five minutes to meditate by _____.

Today, I will "see the tornadoes" created by others and try not to get blown around by them by _____.

Today, I will set a boundary with another person's inappropriate behavior by _____.

Today, I will start my day with prayer by _____.

Today, I will practice being in the eye of the storm by _____.

Today, I will re-establish a relationship with my spiritual beliefs by _____.

Today, I will _____.

Chapter Fifty
Mind-Body-*Spirit*

Happiness is like a butterfly. The more you chase it the more it eludes you.

The other day, I watched our young daughter trying to catch a butterfly in our backyard. She tried and she tried, but she never caught the beautiful, yet elusive butterfly.

Most adults are trying just as hard to "catch" happiness. We try by buying new clothes or a new car. We try by eating too many sweets. We try by running to a new relationship. But happiness still eludes us.

American essayist Agnes Repplier wrote, "It is not easy to find happiness in ourselves, and it is not possible to find it elsewhere." One of the secrets of happiness is to quit looking for it outside of your self. Happiness is a choice found inside of you. For example, choose to be happy with the car that you currently own. It safely transports you from point A to point B. Choose to be happy on a rainy day. You can finish a picture album, a home improvement project, or meditate for a longer period of time. The happiest person doesn't always have the best of everything. She just makes the most of everything that comes her way.

C. L. James wrote this nice analogy in *On Happiness*: "A big cat saw a little cat chasing its tail and asked, 'Why are you chasing your tail so?' Said the kitten, 'I have learned that the best thing for a cat is happiness, and that happiness is my tail. Therefore, I am chasing it and when I catch it, I shall have happiness.' Said the old cat, 'My son, I, too, have paid attention to the problems of the universe. I, too, have judged that happiness is my tail. But, I have noticed that whenever I chase after it, it keeps running away from me, and when I go about my business, it just seems to come after me wherever I go."

Venerable Buddhist Lama Gendun Rinpoche wrote something similar: "Only our searching for happiness prevents us from seeing it. It's like a vivid rainbow which you pursue without ever catching... Happiness cannot be found through great effort and willpower, but is already present in open relaxation and letting go" (Paradox Thirty-six).

Viktor Frankl, the great Austrian psychiatrist and survivor of the Auschwitz concentration camp, said that "Happiness cannot be pursued, it must ensue...as an unintended side effect of one's personal dedication to a cause greater than oneself." Frankl's experiences taught him that one cannot catch happiness, but by getting outside of oneself and being connected to something greater and other-oriented, happiness will follow. Similarly, Nobel Peace Prize winner, physician, and philosopher Albert Schweitzer said, "I don't know what your destiny will be, but the one thing I do know; the only ones among you who will be really happy are those who have sought and found how to serve."

Many people think they will find happiness once they retire, or reach a new income bracket, or during their next vacation. The fallacy of this belief system is that happiness is based on external circumstances. It is as if happiness is a destination. The opposite is true. Happiness is found within the process. For example, the process of getting ready for a vacation can be a royal pain or a fun venture. For happiness to occur, start your preparation early so the packing isn't stressful. Months before you leave, create some family community and look at vacation brochures together. Bring games for the car. All of these strategies will allow for a happier journey. It's your choice.

One truth of life is that life is not a trip—one never arrives. Life is a journey—one that takes many different twists and turns. We might not have consciously chosen every one of the roads, but the choice is ours on what kind of journey it will be. Choose happiness and your life will be more joyful and much bigger.

Today, I will choose happiness by _____.
Today, I will see life as a journey by _____.
Today, I will find happiness within the process of something I do by _____.
Today, I will be aware if I look for happiness internally or externally by _____

Today, I will let go of one external way I thought would bring me happiness by _____.
Today, I will be aware that happiness "just seems to come after me wherever I go" by _____.
Today, I will _____.

Chapter Fifty-One
Mind-Body-*Spirit*

The most valuable things in life are free.

A newspaper columnist interviewed the ten most financially successful people of a large community. Among many of the themes that were present in each of the people's lives was the consistent statement of wishing they had spent more time with their families. These people had been so busy building their business empires that it left little time for their spouses and children.

Hindsight is 20-20. Only in retrospect could they see that relationships with loved one, conversations about daily events, and sharing lives together are more valuable than societal positions, net worth, and sizes of cars and homes.

A paradigm shift that is core to living this paradoxical truth is to realize that we are spiritual beings who are having a human experience. We are not human beings who have spiritual experiences. One way we know this to be true is to realize that the spiritual realm of love, forgiveness, and serenity are much more valuable than the earthy, material realm of possessions and status.

By the second to last chapter of this book, we now know "both-and" thinking is the healthiest and most functional way to create a big life. Most of us want a workable automobile, *and* after the car ride, isn't the walk in the park with a friend worthwhile too? A house or apartment is necessary for our physical existence. *And* isn't an evening inside playing board games with family members just as important?

The Bible states that "...the fruit of the Spirit is love, joy, peace, patience, kindness, goodness, faithfulness, gentleness, self-control...". We forget that these are always available when we get stuck in the material world. If we practice breaking the chains of possessions (Paradox Nineteen) and our occupation (Paradox Twenty-one), these wonderful, *free* gifts are available to each and every one of us.

America has moved from producing the goods people need to producing needs for the goods we make. We have allowed advertisers to have way too much influence over us. Children see advertisements of sugary cereal and ask their parents for it in the grocery aisle. Teenagers see advertisements where athletes promote a particular shoe, and they spend their whole paycheck to buy those shoes. Adults see advertisements of sleeker cars, sexier perfume, or the latest electronic gadgets, and they buy these goods thinking they will feel better about them selves. Sadly, consumerism will never buy happiness. It will only perpetuate looking for acceptance outside of one self—which will never happen.

The season of Christmas creates an environment where our true nature is lived more fully. We are more likely to create community, share presents, laugh, smile, and help those who are less fortunate. All these things feel good—because they flow from our genuine character. Charles Dickens said, "I will honor Christmas in my heart and try to keep it all the year."

May we all accept this challenge. Why shouldn't we—it's free! And, it will create a bigger world for you because you won't be chained down by possessions.

Today, I will re-examine the priorities in my life.

Today, I will acknowledge a "chain" that is holding me back from my true nature and release myself from it.

Today, I will learn from others and spend more time with family and friends.

Today, I will invest more time in free things.

Today, I will cultivate the gifts from God.

Today, I will start to change my paradigm and see myself as a spiritual being.

Today, I will _____.

Chapter Fifty-Two
Mind-Body-Spirit

The whole is greater than the sum of its parts.

We all have many parts to our lives. For example, Mohandas Gandhi was a citizen of India, husband, social reformist, weaver, vegetarian, peace activist, and lawyer. By dissecting his life and looking at the different parts, we do not comprehend the whole essence and full scope of his life. We would not understand why he was given the name Mahatma, which means "great soul."

Drunk drivers have killed many innocent people. These terrible tragedies have left behind thousands of grieving parents. One mother wanted to stop these senseless deaths and created Mothers Against Drunk Drivers. By bringing together the different parents (parts), the organization of MADD became a powerful national movement (whole) that was instrumental in raising the drinking age in all fifty states.

There is not much utility and power in the separate parts of someone or something. When the different parts are consciously brought together, creating an interdependence in their actions, a much bigger and grander end result occurs. For example, all the parts in the grandfather clock are essentially useless until they are integrated with the other parts. The oboe can play beautiful music by itself. But when combined with the rest of the orchestra, a symphony is created.

The synergy of bringing the parts together provides the impetus to move forward in a more functional manner. While each individual makes a difference with his or her vote, an organized lobbying group is more powerful. One person picking up litter does improve our environment. A civic club or group of friends "Adopting a Highway" makes a bigger impact.

This paradoxical truth is even true with raising consciousness. Ken Keyes, Jr., wrote *The Hundredth Monkey*, which reports about a study of Japanese monkeys. On Koshima Island, a group of scientists watched a young monkey learn a new way of cleaning a raw sweet potato. Many other monkeys of this island learned this cultural innovation. A few years later, the scientists noticed that suddenly, there was a significant jump in the number of monkeys washing their sweet potatoes. *And*, this habit spontaneously jumped over the sea to other islands. Troops of monkeys on these islands were now washing their sweet potatoes! The scientists theorized that when a critical mass achieves a certain awareness, this may be communicated "mind to mind." The exact number of needed parts may vary, but when the "Hundredth Monkey...tunes-in to a new awareness, a field (the whole) is strengthened so that this awareness reaches almost everyone!"

Every individual has the potential to be both a saint and a sinner. Everyone needs to be aware of *all* of their different "parts," make healthy choices, which will strengthen their whole self in a saintly manner. This means tending to the mind, body, and spirit. Not being conscious and awake might create a person who is divided and segmented who would live in a dysfunctional manner.

Either way—positive or negative—the whole will be greater than the sum of its parts. This is true with groups. When an individual joins an organization and helps with its cause, the overall effort of the group is strengthened. The synergy of the members makes the group greater than all of its members. This is also true for the entire species. Learning, healing, forgiving, and growing, will strengthen the whole of humanity. Lethargy, hostility, and apathy weaken the whole. The human race is at a crucial point. Your "part" is very important...because what you add to the "whole" is of the utmost importance. Let's make big lives for you, me, and everyone else.

Today, I will add my talents to a group. Specifically, I will _____.

Today, I will become more fully aware of my different parts. Specifically, I will _____.

Today, I will read something that will "stretch" me. Specifically, I will _____.

Today, I will be aware of creating synergy by _____.

Today, I will join a group in whose mission I believe. Specifically, I will _____.

Today, I will add to the healthiness of humanity by _____.

Today, I will _____.